BEHIND THE MAKEUP OF A LEADING LADY

Darlene L. Hart, Collaborator
Rose Godlock, Tamika Parran,
Tiffany Bryan, Adrian Partlow,
Vondale Mack, Patricia Jackson, Michelle Limes

Copyright © 2015 DL Hart Enterprises

All rights reserved. This book is protected under the copyright laws of the United States of America. No portion of this book may be reproduced in any form, without the written permission of the publisher. Permission may be granted on request.

DL Hart Enterprises is not responsible for any content or determination of work. All information is solely considered as the point of view of each author.

ISBN: 0692566449
ISBN-13: 978-0692566442

DEDICATION

This book is dedicated to our Husband's and our children who loved and supported us through this journey. Thank you for being faithful in cheering us on to the finish line and for being our reason behind everything we do. Thank you for pushing us everyday to be better servants for the Kingdom of God, better wives and mothers. Because of your love, support, and prayers we were able to find the person God created us to be. We thank God everyday for finding us worthy of sharing this life with you.

We Love you to Life,

Us

CONTENTS

		Acknowledgments	I
1	Darlene L. Hart	Defeating Goliath Within	Pg 3
2	Rose Godlock	Something Special	Pg 24
3	Tamika Parran	Confidence Course	Pg 36
4	Tiffany Bryan	Our Leading Lady	Pg 52
5	Adrian Partlow	I Never Gave You Permission	Pg 66
6	Vondale Mack	The Allure of Unclean Honey	Pg 77
7	Patricia Jackson	A Most Deadly Disease	Pg 93
8	Michelle Limes	Getting Back to My Happy Place	Pg 106
		Also Available	Pg 107

THANK YOU

To our family, friends, and church family for your love, support and your prayers. Thank you for encouraging us to be who God created us to be.

With Love Always,

Us

Darlene L. Hart
Christian Tabernacle Church of God
2033 11th St. NW
Washington, DC 20001
DL Hart Enterprises
www.DLHartent.com
Admin@DLHartent.com
(240)377-1547

Darlene L. Hart affectionately known as Lady D is a Preacher, Teacher, Entrepreneur, and a personal cheerleader to many. She is the creator and visionary for the Behind the Makeup project. Lady D is on a mission for the body of Christ to remove their mask and live authentically as God created them. Under this movement Lady D brings together women from various backgrounds in ministry to share their testimony of hope and inspiration. The first book called Behind the Makeup, featured 7 women Darlene Hart, Christal Wooten, Tracy Orie, Tonita Bell, Nya Small, Donnica Crossland and Lauraline Gregory all women who serve in ministry. Her second book in this series is Behind The Makeup of a Leading Lady which features 8 women including her. They are Patricia Jackson, Rose Godlock, Tamika Parran, Michelle Limes, Adrian Partlow, and Vondale Mack who all serve as the Leading Lady in their ministry. Lady Darlene is eager to release her much anticipated book, called 6 Months to Life, a 183-day guide to releasing the past and moving forward into the life you were meant to live. 6 Months to Life is a daily inspirational activity book that was created to encourage people to take active steps in changing their life. Lady D has also completed another life goal in July 2014, which was starting a Foundation named Ensuring The Future, an organization geared to empowering families that are suffering from drug and alcohol addiction.

Lady D was trained, and licensed by the late Bishop William F. Hart Jr., on January 6, 2002. God has ordained Lady D to be a servant and Women's Pastor for Women of the Word Ministry. She is an example of endurance and strength and believes in the power of prayer. Lady D has surrendered her life to God and the leading of the Holy Spirit accepting the call to stand alongside her husband and serve as Pastor and First Lady of the Christian Tabernacle Church of God located in Washington, DC.

Lady D is married to Pastor Kevin T. Hart Sr. and together the Lord has blessed them with five amazing and gifted children Kierra, Khiyana, Kailynn, Kevin Jr. and Kaleb. Lady D believes that every family has the ability to thrive if they keep their faith in God and a prayer on their lips. Lady D is always striving to be an example of God before all mankind and echo Him throughout the earth. It is her desire to see men and women live out their dreams and walk in their purpose.

Lady D believes she can do all things through Christ who gives her strength and she is committed to stand on the word of God despite the obstacles that rise up against her. To her amazement God strategically repositioned her life and she now declares to all who will listen that "You never know what God is up to, but it's all for your good!"

DEFEATING GOLIATH WITHIN
Learning To Trust Again

Webster's Definition of Trust: Trust is defined as firm belief in the reliability, truth, ability, or strength of someone or something.

For me trust is crucial in relationships and once it's broken, all bets are off; it would become a major deal breaker for me. It does not matter whether it's business or personal, I need to be able to trust the person I am dealing with. There are many who believe once trust is broken it can never be repaired and the relationship is over. After leaning on the Lord for wisdom, I now believe it's possible to trust again, but I have to admit, it will require a lot of honesty and work. If you seek to regain someone's trust, you have to be completely upfront with them and you have to be careful not to damage the relationship, or it will reinjure what you worked hard to repair. It would be like ripping the scab off of a sore that started to heal and you open it back up again. Waiting for a scar to re-heal seems like it takes longer to heal the next time. Trust is a difficult emotion to overcome because it deals with the heart and mind concurrently. What you believe and how you feel become intertwined. The mind now believes what the heart has accepted. You have trained yourself to think, act, and behave a certain way. It is the old adage that says to forgive but don't forget concept. You certainly have to retrain your mind to believe all things are possible and destroy the mindset that there are limits on what you are capable of doing. It is not an easy fix, and at times you may feel as though you will never be able to regain trust again, but it is definitely fixable. Trust is tied to prior experiences of hurt and betrayal. Whenever a person has lost trust in any significant relationship like parents, a spouse, a relative, or close friend, anything that conveys the same behavior, or action of a prior experience will give you cause to be alarmed and your defense mechanism will rise up. For example, if you have been in a relationship and the other person cheated on you, if you have not resolved your issues with from the past the next relationship you enter into, if that person stays out late or frequently misses your calls, you will assume they are cheating on you. For me, I developed a negative attitude and my guard would immediately go up. The wall became my protection, a security blanket from all the potential pain I might possibly experience. The problem with that way of living is you are not allowing yourself to develop any meaningful relationships because you are always guarded by what might happen.

If I found out someone lied to me, it would be hard for me to ever believe one word out of their mouth from that moment forward. I did not trust anyone, not just those who had offended me, but almost everyone around me. Life tossed me a few curveballs I was not able to hit out of the park. I had to learn that trust was not a deal breaker, nor do I have to operate under the premise that you can forgive but not forget. Operating under this type of mindset always leaves room for you to hold onto the offense and the underlying issue leads back to you not having trust in someone. Not being able to trust people will show up in all areas of your life, and it stunts your own growth both personally and professionally. Everyone has a giant they must defeat, mines just happen to be within me.

David came face to face with an opportunity to defeat a Giant in his life, and for his friends, family, and co-laborers lives. (1 Samuel 17) He proved that any giant could be defeated with a little effort. It does not require a lot of skill and knowledge; just a willing heart. No matter how long the giant has been hanging around and despite its size much like David, we all have to face off with something that has the capability to destroy us. Your Goliath could be adultery, fornication, stealing, or lying. Or it could be that you were abandoned, hurt, molested, beaten, or a form of sickness. You may be at a crossroad in your life, one that will require you to make a critical decision to move forward or stand still and impede your own progress. You can either live with Goliath or defeat your giant within. I pray you will remove the barriers preventing you from growing.

David slayed Goliath, eliminating what stood between him and his destiny. He was not intimidated by the size of his competitor nor was he concerned whether the slingshot he carried would be enough. David made a conscious decision to conquer and destroy his opponent and that's exactly what he did. We have to be intentional about our desires to eradicate what is keeping us from living the full life that the Lord came to give to us. (John 10:10)

Foundation

I had roadblocks in my life. I could not understand why I was always living on the verge of a breakthrough but never actually cracking through the surface. I was experiencing minimal blessings, but there was nothing extraordinary. I was doing everything I was taught to do pray, fast, and study the Word of God, not to mention every time the doors of the church were opened I was there and still I had roadblocks. Despite the tithes and offerings I was giving, I still was going nowhere fast.

I felt as though everyone around me was receiving what they prayed for and they were being blessed beyond what they sought God for, yet here I was standing at the door watching from the outside, but never being able to walk in and be a partaker of the blessings being handed out. What was I doing wrong? What was I missing? The Bible says in Hebrews 11:6 And without faith it is impossible to please God, because anyone who comes to him must believe that he exists and that he rewards those who earnestly seek him. My inability to trust people caused me to lose faith in God, and not only had I lost my faith; I doubted God would do it. I believed God was able to do it, He could do it, I just did not believe He would do it for me. With all I was doing to build my relationship with God, I still missed that I doubted Him. I didn't really understand what having faith and pleasing God meant. This meant I also didn't realize He was a rewarder of those who diligently seek Him. (Hebrews 11:6) I believed the worse would happen, a complete and total pessimist. Despite the prayers, I still did not expect to receive what I asked for. I would only rely on what I could see, touch, and hear and even that could be suspect. The impossible was limited by my own belief. I was used to being disappointed, so without realizing, I stopped expecting anything else.

After experiencing a few devastating situations, I became intentional about developing my relationship with the Lord. I began to feast off of the Word of God, and the more I read the Bible, the more I understood who I was. I needed to understand why I did not have the capacity to trust anyone so; I read every scripture I could find on trust. I began to rely on the scripture to reshape my thoughts and point me in the direction God desired for me to walk in and I dismiss what others thought I should be doing. When I began to feel uneasy about a business decision or a person I was dealing with, I would quote Psalms 20:7 Some trust in chariots and some in horses, but we trust in the name of the LORD our God. It would just remind me that as long as I put my trust in the Lord, He would never lead me astray. The Bible holds many promises I relied on in times of confusion. My greatest revelation was understanding how I'd somehow believed I was suffering because the Lord was repaying me for all of the mistakes I made in the past. As if God was waiting for me to give my life to Him to destroy my marriage, stress me out with the overdue bills, lack of finances, a discriminating boss, and a life filled with horrible nightmares. I held God accountable for the actions of man. In tough times we have the options to seek God for answers or take matters into our own hands and try to fix it our way. Free will allows us to choose the direction we want to take. God is not going to force Himself on us. Therefore, we must trust Him to change our heart, heal our wounds, and comfort us in tough times.

Trust for me meant everything had to happen the way I planned; people would show up for me as I expected them too. Pretty much I had to be in complete control of my life the entire time. The world is unpredictable, there is no way to be in total control all of the time, and it became clear to me that I was not living at all, I merely existed. Now, I had to choose to live fully in each moment, good or bad I needed to experience life. That was my fork in the road; one led to a full life and the other led to death; I no longer wanted to be alive living a dead ended life. I decided it was time for me to live!

Eye shadow

I took a good long look at myself; it may sound cliché only because people say they do it, but most really haven't taken a genuine assessment of their selves. It's necessary to examine yourself, according to the Word of God we should judge ourselves to see if we have genuine faith. *2 Corinthians 13:5 examine yourselves to see whether you are in the faith; test yourselves. Do you not realize that Christ Jesus is in you--unless, of course, you fail the test?* Sometimes we claim to have faith, but when it is tested and tried, we find we have worried when we should have been assured God was in control. Or maybe there were moments when we've tried to figure out a solution on our own instead of waiting for the Lord to answer our prayer. It is in the testing we find out if we really have faith in God or not.

One morning while sitting in my living room, I saw a commercial for Lego's and I thought: When was the last time I saw a Lego commercial? I reminisced about how I played for hours with those things and imagined how frustrated I became because I was unable to make something out of those pieces laying all over the floor. Every year there was a new Lego game that hit the stores for Christmas and I never failed to buy them for my children. No matter how busy I was, I would always take a moment to play Lego's with the kids trying to make something out of nothing. My children were fascinated with creating different things out of the assorted shapes and sizes of various colored blocks. Those pieces were scattered all of over the floor and eventually they would come up with a plane, a large building, and even a car. There was nothing you couldn't construct with just a little imagination. As I revisited my experience with the Lego's and the things I made or witnessed others create, I realized that they transformed what looked to be broken pieces into something wonderful. I was enjoying my moment of reflection when the Lord kept saying repeatedly, Lego. The Lord was not trying to get me to remember the games I played with those crazy looking pieces, He was trying to get me to pay attention to the word so over and over; I heard a resounding Lego, and finally, it clicked, I got it. It was the message I needed to focus on and it was to let go! Pick up the pieces of my life; create something beautiful out of what appears to be broken and let go of everything that occurred in the past! I attached myself to the pain so deeply that I could only focus on what I did not like or what happened to me. I rehearsed hurtful conversations and incidents over and over until I would end up being just as furious as I had been when it happened. I was content living in a state of agony, because without it, I didn't know what to feel. I was used to something going wrong, so I refused to get my hopes up only to be let down again. Now the Lord is telling me I needed to let go if I wanted to change my life, I had to let go of the negative emotions and focus on the positive. I wanted to have peace in my home, restoration in my marriage, and I wanted my children to grow up in a healthy environment and to have all of that, I would have to make some alterations to me.

The Lord reminded me that I permitted the pain, and the broken, scattered pieces of hurt and anger to control me. So I refocused all of my energy in discovering who God created me to be. It was my own personal excavation mission and I had to start digging out from under the years of pain and to get to know the real me.

God began to break down the way I saw myself, and the way I looked at others. I held people responsible for my pain. The more time I took to study the Word of God, the more I understood the lies I told myself. I began to dissect every scripture I read, including the commentary. One of my favorite scriptures that I would recite daily was Hebrews Proverbs 3:5, 6 *Trust in the LORD with all your heart and do not lean on your own understanding. In all your ways acknowledge Him, and He will make your paths straight.* I needed to yield myself to Him and allow Him to direct my path. This scripture is a reflection of my daily prayer to the Lord to guide me and direct my path that I may follow His will for my life. I may not always understand His will, but as long as I am following His lead, I knew He would guide me to a life of happiness and the love I desired.

Lipstick

Just before I got married, I found out my husband had an addiction to narcotics. It was not something I was not familiar with since in my home my parents barely even drank alcohol. My Dad may have a few beers here and there but we rarely saw him drinking in the house, he was the kind of person that kept a cooler in the back of his van. My family was very good about keeping adult things away from the children. It would be years later that I'd find out there were people in my family who also had an addiction to drugs and alcohol. So, naturally my knowledge about drugs was limited to marijuana, which was very basic compared to cocaine or crack. However, I still decided to marry him because I thought our love was stronger than anything. Our daughter Kierra, was almost one- year-old and I wanted her to have a good relationship with her father. I remember thinking that his love for his daughter and me would miraculously change him and he wouldn't want to use drugs and alcohol anymore. How naïve of me...right? Of course it was to believe you could love away a person's addiction was quite ridiculous. Nonetheless, I stuck it out because when we met we had so many things in common; we knew we were meant to be together because it was things we decided we wanted years before we met. Both Kevin and I were raised by parents that were still married and living in the same household. We were amazed that we finally met someone who still had parents that were not divorced. It was hard meeting someone whose Dad lived in the house with them, or had never been married. A person who still had both parents at home was rare and that was something we both wanted to give our children should we ever had one. We loved to be around family, and we enjoyed hanging out laughing at absolutely nothing. When I found out I was pregnant, I decided I would stay with him because we shared similar goals and we came from the same background. We wanted the same things in life. I also decided early in life that I did not want to have children with different fathers. I only wanted to deal with one person and if that relationship did not work out, then I had no plans on having anymore children. It was a promise I made to myself and I kept my promises. We did not plan the pregnancy and I guess we did not plan the marriage. We did however, plan the wedding. Past that, there was no preparation for me to be a wife. I did not really comprehend what being a wife really meant. However, I knew I wanted to be married, and have ten children.

I wanted to be a fun wife and mother. As reality set in, I knew the life I dreamed of was pretty much that it was a dream. The truth was I had difficulty wrapping my mind around taking care of a family and receiving little appreciation for it. I had no clue that I was accepting the responsibility to help Kevin overcome his addiction. I was now known as a co-addict. To my surprise, I had unconsciously decided that I would put myself last. Last, after everything else, especially his true obsession and only love, the drugs.

After we married, he tried for a quick moment to stay clean. He would stay out until the early morning hours, or he would not come home at all. Sometimes, I would not see him for three or more days. After a while, he would purposely start arguments so he could leave and blame me for him not being able to get past his addiction because I was always fussing or mad. I did not know what to think, I tried it all, but nothing held his attention long enough to make him stay sober. The late night knocks at the door, and the rocks thrown at the window worried and frustrated me. I began to receive calls from random people demanding money. I became a nervous wreck and I watched everyone around me laugh at the crazy things he was doing in the neighborhood. I started becoming so afraid to go in his old neighborhood because I did not want anyone to attack me for something he had done. I would never allow my children out of my sight; they were not allowed to spend the night over anyone's house, because I was fearful that something could happen to them. To be on the safe side, I always kept the children with me.

Despite his addiction, people loved my husband, I loved him. He was everyone's favorite person. There were a few people who told me to leave him, but ironically there were not that many, at least that I really trusted to be honest with me. By this time, I was emotionally broken and I trusted no one anyway, so whatever I was told went in one ear and left through the other. In my eyes, everyone wanted to hurt me, lie to me, and did not care about me and what I was going through as his wife. All the questions and concerns were about my husband and how he is doing or reminders of what I needed to do to help him. Meanwhile, no one ever asked how I was doing or tried to find out if I needed anything. With all of the scriptures people quoted to me about love, you would have thought at least one of them would have thought about me or asked how the kids were doing with all that was happening with their Dad.

People somehow believe kids are ignorant to their surroundings or that they would forget as they got older. Children are always being taught, even if you send them out of the room; they are still able to hear how disagreements are being handled. My children could always sense when something was happening with their father. They always asked a lot of questions and I felt like I owed them the truth. I shared with them in moderation and on a case-by-case basis. Every time he came home and then left again, sometimes for days at a time, it forced me to be honest with them so they would not be confused about anything they were witnessing. While I was worrying about the children developing harsh feelings toward their dad, I was the one who was harboring bitterness and resentment.

I was taught not to bad mouth the absent parent because you do not want the children to be upset with their parent. I believe we create delusional people when we allow them to make up their own endings to what they witnessed instead of giving them clarity about things they could not possible understand. You can tell the truth in love without bashing the parent. I tried to be neutral. I told them the truth so they would not follow in his footsteps and also become an addict. I had friends who ended up using drugs because they saw their parents using. What kind of parent would I be if they ended up abusing drugs? Then people would say I was a bad parent. Being a mother caused me to live a different way, I wanted them to love their dad and boy did they love his stinking drawls as his mother used to say. That is because I taught them the truth in a way that caused them to love and honor the man, but not the sin.

Fast-forward a few years, I had now left my husband several times, we were in the on again off again stage of our relationship. I moved and started over so I thought, and filed for divorce, even went to court to see it all the way through this time. To my surprise, I would eventually be right back in his arms, but this time I would be in control. Control was my daily motivation. I knew where my kids were, who they were with, and they were not allowed to do anything I did not approve. Fear ruled my world and theirs. I had to be in charge of everything to be comfortable. I became the ultimate control freak because I did not like anything to happen by surprise. I didn't like surprise drop-ins to my house, so I did not tell people where I lived, only my family. I really could not let anyone make a decision without me being involved. I was only comfortable when I held all the cards. My husband could not have his own car because having a car meant he could disappear easy and go to places I knew nothing about. Taking our children with him was not allowed, because an urge could hit him and he may drop them off anywhere. Nothing ever happened to my children. I worried myself trying to prevent something that was only occurring in my head. This became a normal life for me and I was under the delusion that I was not the one who with the problem. I had now backed myself and my children into a place where no one could help us if they wanted to.

I had become comfortable with the thorn in my flesh and did not even recognize it was there. It was my reality and the only way I knew to be safe; no sudden moves, and no accidental sounds. I am in control of it all! Living like this was not really living; it was building a wall around myself and isolating myself from the world. I did not realize that I blocked, pushed away, and tore up every relationship in my way. I pretended to be strong even when I felt like I was going to crumble to pieces. I became intrigued with people who were living their dreams and were not afraid to take a risk. While I watched from the sidelines, they were playing full force in the game of life. They showed up dressed and ready to get in the game, and not just to play, but to win.

I finally realized that no one was going to show up to save me and change my life. I had to take action and handle it myself. We sit in workshops, church services, read self help books, and listen to motivational speeches and we still do nothing. The reason we do not see any effects from all of the information we've received is because we don't do anything with it. W e need to apply the things we have heard, read, and were taught.

My trust was shattered from all of life's events that popped over time. I remember when my supervisor told me, he would "watch my back." I was an armed guard for many years, I was not making much money and the hours were the worse. I needed a new job with better hours and more money. I wound up being switched to a new site with a whole new group of people. I was put on night shift and no matter how many hours I worked, I still could not meet the amount of bills that were piled on the table. Eventually, I ended up working double shifts to make ends meet, until one of my co-workers came in and resigned and told everyone about this new company that was starting and they were paying really well. He encouraged all of us to apply because he was just hired as the Captain of the company and he wanted all of us to come and be on his team. One of the benefits of having a special police officer license was you can change your license over to another company at will. There were several security companies in the Washington DMV area and all of them were hiring at one time or another. So I ran and quickly changed my license over and began working for this brand new agency. I was hired as the office manager that handled contracts and any other task that was handed down to me. I had a sweet schedule too. I worked Monday through Friday from 8 a.m. in the morning until 4 p.m. in the afternoon. I no longer had to work nights and weekends and on top of that I got a raise in my salary. I was literally skipping to work everyday and excited to have a job that I did not have to be in the field, I could sit in the office and work in peace.

Well peace soon ended when the Lieutenant also started working in the office with the Captain and me. Everyday, she would for no reason at all find something to complain about. I could not do anything right in her eyes and she was going to make sure I knew it. If the Captain did not intervene she would have found a reason to terminate me. The Captain came to me and informed me that she wanted to fire me, but he would cover my back to ensure I would not be fired, because he knew I was a single mother, and I needed my job. So here I was secure in my position and still trying to befriend a woman who had no desire to be a friend to anyone. As the months passed, the Captain and I became good friends. I talked to him and his wife about a lot of things because they were Christian counselors at their church. They were an older couple, with two small children. They were fun-loving and were always joking around with each other. The way I wanted to be in my marriage. They gave me the perfect advice and did not mind if I called them anytime of the day or night. The only problem was the Captain began to involve himself in my personal life all of the time. He did not mind questioning where I was and what I was doing all of the time.

He began to send the Lieutenant out of the office everyday for hours at a time. He walked in my office and confessed that he was interested in being more than a friend to me. I was really confused because he and his wife appeared to be happy. I thought he was kidding, so I brushed him off. That seemed to make him more interested, because he started pulling on my arm trying to put his arms around me and no matter how much I resisted, he continued to pursue. My coworker came back to the office and he left me alone, and I thought; wow, what would have happened if she had not come back to the office? I left the office that day worried about what happened, but I said nothing to no one. How would I tell anyway? The next day when I arrived at work, the Captain apologized and we went on with our day. He blamed it on some ridiculous reason and left it alone and so did I. A few days passed, and of course he pursued me all over again, and this time with more force and he would continue to behave this way for weeks. One day, the Captain said I needed to work on Saturday because they needed me to help with some reports and it was mandatory that I did this assignment. I could use the extra cash, and working alone in the office on a Saturday was just what I needed to get away from the crazy Lieutenant who fussed all day and the Captain who tried to force himself on me almost daily. I showed up at work and started working on the reports when the Captain walked in and marched to his office. He stayed in there for a while and I thought great he was not up to his shenanigans today and I could finish and go home. After a couple of hours, he came to my office and started rubbing on my shoulders, I jumped from my seat and began yelling at him that this time he was not going to keep messing with me. He grabbed my arms, and pinned me down, I wrestled with him frantically, he saw the tears in my eyes and still he would not stop trying to force himself on me. He was trying to rape me in the office and it would be my word against his. How could I have been so foolish to trust someone so disgusting? He was a father of two young toddlers and he had been married for years. A Deacon and counselor at the church he's served in for years and here he was now trying to rape me. Finally, after a few minutes I broke free, grabbed my things and left the office. I went home, and tried to think of what to do about the horrible incident, but I needed my job. Keeping silent all this time has gotten me nowhere. I was afraid to speak up, and I was afraid to keep quiet. My arms and legs were sore from him pinning me down trying to force my legs open. I screamed, but who could have heard me, I was in the basement office in a building that was closed on the weekends. How could I have been so stupid not to see this coming and to even put my trust in a man that could be so deceitful?

When I returned to work he apologized as usual and I told him that I was never going to sleep with him and because I refused to have sex with him, he sent me to work on a post in a rough neighborhood, Potomac Gardens. I had not worked this site before and I was at a loss, why had he sent me on site, they were not short-handed or anything. After a while, he called me back to the office and began threatening to change my work site because he did not want to work with me anymore. Of course, he knew I did not want to work in a rough neighborhood, nor did I want to lose my schedule, so he used that as a tactic to get me to conform to what he wanted. I told him he was only doing that because I would not have sex with him, he denied it of course, but I knew the truth. He gave me a few days to think it over and then he tried his hand again, and this time I was tired of the stress of having to physically fight him off, so I contacted the owner of the company and told him what was happening to me and he scheduled a meeting with us both. The owner we called Boss, he actually sounded concerned and I believed he was truly going to step in and make him stop or fire him. Security was a man's field of work, so they thought, and they were about to prove to me just how much they were in charge. After the meeting, we went back to work and a few days went passed and Boss called me into his office and said he did not want to subject me to having to work with him in the office. Since he could prove anything happened he did not trust that nothing would happen to me if I continued to work with him so he was going to have to move me somewhere safe. It was his word against mine, he did not want me to be at risk in case it was true. Which meant he would have to find me a new location to work; and that meant I now had to give up my schedule and he put me back on a post, and the Captain got a slap on the wrist. I was eventually terminated without cause; I was told they did not have enough work to keep me on schedule, so they had to let me go. Now here I am. The man that said he would have my back only had it if he could do it standing directly behind me. The man not only tried to rape me, he took away what was important to me, my job, the way I provided for my children, and my reputation. That man started spreading rumors about me throughout the company, saying I was his mistress and I was fired for harassing him to be with me. I never saw that man again, but armed guards moved from company to company, which meant I had to relive the hurt and the rumors repeatedly whenever I worked with one of them and was questioned why I was fired.

I decided I would never put myself in that situation again and/or trust people just because their life looked happy. If a person claimed to have my back, they had to prove it and not with words. The problem is trusting someone is not about being able to visually see a perfect supportive person, it's about letting people be themselves and seeing them for who they are, good or bad. Who a person is, will eventually show up for you and they will prove to you who they really are. That is the reason we should never rush into a relationship with anyone in any way until we have established a relationship with him or her. I beat myself up for years because I allowed people to get close enough to me to hurt me or deceive me. I was not a newcomer to hurt and pain from people and years later after my husband and I renewed our vows, I struggled with trusting him because of his past and those who hurt me in my past. The following years would prove to be a test until the Lord began dealing with me on the place I allowed hurt and pain to reside. The secrets I kept and the things that hurt me that I acted like did not bother me. Trust wasn't about anyone else but me. It was really about me trusting myself to make wise decisions. It was time for me to change and of course once you determine you are ready to change you are going to be faced with a series of challenges in the area you are working on. I believe it is a test to see if you are serious about the change you seek after. A few days later, I began having car trouble and I took my car to the shop. Isn't it funny how God uses the simplest things to get our attention? I usually ride with the music loud and I rarely turn it down until I pull into my driveway. Well, for some reason, on this day I got into my car and turned everything off and just began to drive. I rode around all day in complete and total silence. I needed to get in a quiet place so I could think clearly without any distractions and the open road seems to do that for me. I was driving my car when it started making this crazy noise, I thought maybe something got caught under my car or something was stuck in my tire. I thought if I just kept driving, it would pop out and I could keep going. It never changed, so I went home and decided that I would call the mechanic in the shopping center by my home and he would take care of it. I called and he gave me some outrageous price and a long list of things wrong with my car. Things that I did not have any clue were wrong. Now we all have heard about those mechanics that take advantage of women by jacking up the price so they end up overpaying for work they never needed. I decided to pick up my car and take it somewhere else, and this time the mechanic gave me a new list of problems and when I told him I just left another shop, and he did not find those problems, he looked at my estimate and said, "Oh no, I did not find those things." He looked again and said, "Yeah some of this needs to be fixed as well." I knew he was lying and what he saw was dollar symbols and not a mother who had bills and five children to provide for. I wished him well, got into my car and drove my loud clanking car away. When I got home and told my husband what happened, in disbelief he said they know what they're doing and you should just trust them and let them fix your car. I now looked at him like he'd lost his mind. Pay that amount of money for repairs I knew I did not need? Now I am driving in my car for almost two weeks with this crazy sound coming from my car and I could not find one person who would be honest with me and tell me what was wrong with it. As if I had some prior knowledge about fixing a car. I had determined today I would find someone to fix my car and they were going to be honest and only charge me for the repairs I needed. Years before I had car trouble and the mechanic told me the labors were part of the reason my bills were high and the higher the bill the more commission he received. That stuck with me forever. I now believe everyone raised their prices so they're commission would be high. I was annoyed and frustrated, but I needed to have my car repaired, it was my only transportation. I prayed, and drove around headed nowhere, I pulled onto the shoulder of the road and prayed again, I pulled out back into traffic and this time, I heard the sound even louder. This time the noise seemed to command my attention as if the Lord showing me through sounds what to listen for. I listened closely. It was a screeching noise, and then the Lord directed me to not just listen, but to pay attention to when the sound occurred. Now I am paying attention to every sound and movement so I would not miss anything. Just then, I realized the only time I heard the noise was when I tried to stop my car. It was my brakes grinding and screeching. It wasn't the engine, and not one of the mechanics I took my car to told me that was the problem. I called my husband on the phone and told him it was my brakes making that noise all of this time, and my husband says, "Oh, I have the perfect guy who can fix brakes and he is really good." This man was a well-established mechanic, I told him I needed my brakes repaired. I spoke confidently, so he would not feel as if he was dealing with an airhead he could mislead into believing anything. Even after I told him what I believed the problem to be, he looked at the car and commenced to explain in grave detail what repairs I needed. I needed rotors, pads, and wheel bearing and a few other miscellaneous things. Nowhere near the list of things the other two men stated, but still more than I was prepared for. I was operating under the belief that I was in control, because I was armed with information and the Lord even revealed to me the problems with the car. I did not even need to hear the report, just how much the repairs were going to cost me. There was no way there were other things I needed to repair. I tried to explain to this mechanic what I knew from my limited amount of knowledge and he was telling me from his extensive background that I needed these things in order for my brakes to be fixed properly. Despite his expertise, I still got in my car and drove away, pulled into my driveway, and my phone rings and the person on the other end begins to complain to me how bad their day was going. Wouldn't you know it? They were talking about how they could not trust their husband to make decisions for their family because of the poor choices he's made in the past and here I am encouraging her to trust him. When I completed the call, I hung up the phone and instantly the conversation replayed in my mind as I was walking in the house. I realized I needed to take my own advice. I prayed and despite the Lord answering my prayers, I still had doubts. Even with the Lord's leading, I still could not make a decision. I DID NOT EVEN TRUST THE LORD! That was a huge revelation for me. I could not make decisions because I did not trust the people, I did not trust what I thought the Lord was showing me about my situation, I did not trust my husband. Again I realize I did not trust myself. The next day I woke up both naturally and spiritually. I took my car to the shop and let the mechanic make the necessary repairs. It was difficult to trust someone I knew nothing about and even pay them. This was a costly lesson to learn. If I had only trusted those who were licensed and trained in areas I knew nothing about, and been obedient to the Lord when He answered the prayers I prayed I would have gotten my car fixed and it would not have cost me extra money from me continuing to ride around with messed up brakes. I caused more damage waiting and all because I could not trust myself to trust someone else. I could not continue to behave in this manner. Everyday we should examine our walk with God. Somehow, we have stopped being honest with ourselves and admitting there are areas in our lives we need help in. Even if it means we have to seek the advice of a counselor or a mentor. We have to always look for ways to make our lives better. If we desire change, we have to be participants in the process to make it happen. There is no magic wand we can wave over our circumstances and watch it transform into what we want. I had too much at stake to remain the same; my family, my relationships were all suffering at my own hands. Trust is not given it is earned, and I had to allow people to be human and make mistakes and trust it was not intentional. Trust was the giant in my life I needed to defeat and until I took out my slingshot and faced it head on, it would be with me forever. I refused to allow that giant to stand in the way of my happiness. Trust is looking past what you see with your natural eye, it's about putting your trust in the right hands. Trust God, He deserves your trust. People are imperfect and can make mistakes however; if you put your faith and trust in God He will not let you down.

Rebuilding The Foundation

If it is your desire to renovate your life, you will have to make the decision from the start to be brutally honest with the person you see everyday in the mirror. Your first move should be to reshape your thoughts. Challenge the lies you have been authorizing yourself to believe. When a thought comes to your mind, do you allow that thought to control you, your mood, how you feel, do you become angry or sad? Do your thoughts sometimes cause you to feel uncomfortable? If so, you should wash your thoughts with the Word of God. Are you living in fear? What does the Bible say about fear? Do you believe you can never forgive someone? You may be still wrestling with mistakes you've made. What does the Bible say about forgiveness? If you are living a life filled with anger, find out what the Bible says about anger. When you begin to challenge your thoughts with the Word of God, you will see many of your thoughts are rooted in deception and was never the way God desired for us to think about yourself or others. Wash your mind with scripture and if what you are thinking does not line up with what the Bible says, then you replace it with the truth in God's Word. When a poor choice or bad thought arises, measure it with the Word and if it is not truth take the thought captive. *2 Corinthians 10:5 we demolish arguments and every pretension that sets itself up against the knowledge of God, and we take captive every thought to make it obedient to Christ. Let's first examine ourselves:*

- ➢ There are things that you have done that have contributed to the person you have become. Sometimes part of the alterations we need to make in our life is the people we keep around us. Some people will never push you to where we need or want to be. It is true Iron sharpens iron (Proverbs 27:17). A good friend will enhance you and make you better; they would never be satisfied with you living a mediocre lifestyle especially if they're not living small. You have to evaluate those who you spend the most amount of your time with and whether or not they are living up to what they want for their own life.

- ➢ Find an accountability partner, someone you trust will hold you accountable to take bold steps to obtaining your dreams. Choose someone that is not afraid to question your commitment to your dreams. It should be someone you've given authority to cheer for your success, challenge your thoughts, question your behavior, criticize and correct you. You should always choose someone that is ok with telling you when you are wrong. Truthfully, a person who agrees with everything you say and do is not someone who has your best interest at heart. No one does everything perfectly all of the time.

- ➢ Memorize three scriptures you can recite to refocus you when you are feeling challenged in your choice area. Since I struggled with trust, I choose scriptures I could draw strength from and remind me who I should put my trust in. Here are three scriptures I recite when I feel uneasy or I have to make a decision to trust someone:

Proverbs 3:5, 6 Trust in the Lord with all thine heart; and lean not unto thine own understanding. In all thy ways acknowledge him, and he shall direct thy paths.

2 Corinthians 10:5 we demolish arguments and every pretension that sets itself up against the knowledge of God, and we take captive every thought to make it obedient to Christ.

1 Corinthians 9:27 but I beat my body and bring it into submission, for fear that by any means, that after I have preached to others, I myself should be rejected.

I kept a spiral notebook and each day I would write down the lies I believed and after each lie I would write the truth from God's word. Then I had a reference point I could revisit whenever I needed to. I was arming myself and developing a daily regimen to help me change my thoughts and rebuild my foundation. Honestly, it helped to set the tone for the day. I used to pick up my phone and read emails, text messages, and social media. It would really bother me if I read something disturbing and it made my day start off in the wrong direction. Instead, every morning before my feet hit the floor, I would thank God for allowing me to see another day. Then I would pray, whenever I am unsure what to pray, I recited the Lord's pray which is the most powerful prayer I know. The Bible says we do not have to go on babbling like a pagan, so there is no need for an hour long prayer because God knows what you need before you have a need (Mathew6:5-8). Let us pray the Lord's Prayer together. The prayer is found in Matthew 6:9-13 (NIV) "This, then, is how you should pray: "Our Father in heaven, hallowed be your name, your kingdom come, your will be done, on earth as it is in heaven. Give us today our daily bread. And forgive us our debts, as we also have forgiven our debtors. And lead us not into temptation, but deliver us from the evil one." To make this prayer more personal, I would change the word us or our and say "I" or "me." Prayer is your time to communicate with your Creator and how can you start a day and not speak to the one who made this day possible?

After my prayer time, I would review my action list which is basically a to do list I write the night before to make sure I handled all of my necessary action items that day. I call it an Action list because it entices me to get active on the daily goals I set for myself. I check off everything I've completed and I transfer whatever is incomplete to the following day. I use a calendar and my IPhone for reminders. I set all sorts of reminders on my IPhone to ensure I keep up with the goals I set for myself. After reviewing my action list, I start my day. Because I now trust my husband to take care of the kids, we now take turns and rotate the responsibility of caring for them and getting them ready for bed or preparing them for school. My husband would take the mornings and get them up and out the door for school and I would take the evening shift making dinner, doing homework, and getting them ready for bed. Then we could each have a break and the weight was not all on me. Even if I am at home, I make sure I am just as involved with my schedule as I am my children's schedule. Most of the time we put ourselves on the back burner to ensure our family needs are met. We have to remember that we are included in the family and are equally entitled to be happy; we don't always have to come after everyone else. I learned to prioritize everyone's needs, including my own.

After prayer and reviewing the plan for the day, I would start my day, which included going to work, but this way I did not feel rushed or off track. The best plan for me was to prepare myself to be successful. That meant I had to guard my thoughts, and what I allowed to have access to me and my spirit by protecting what I watched or read. I could not allow anything to disturb me. Just like everyone else, I am human and I get off track, but when or if I do I don't beat myself up for it. I move at my pace and not others, I choose to be myself and not try to live up to who others feel I should be. Life became so much sweeter for me once I searched myself and realized where I was holding myself back. I wanted to live and not just exist. I invite you to take your own excavation mission, if you notice you are stuck and living a stagnant life, it's time for you shift your program and try something new. It is always a good to examine your walk and see where you line up. Find the Goliaths in your life that may have been laying dormant within you and defeat it. Accepting that you have issue's you still have to deal with does not mean there is something wrong with you, it means you realize you are a work in progress. We are all striving to be better people and it takes being real with yourself and saying I need help, I need to change. It's ok to admit you want to be a better version of yourself. God is pleased with us when we desire to work on ourselves and take action to better ourselves so we may serve Him fully as He designed us to. Life is so much better when you live free from the giants we have become comfortable living with. Let's us defeat our own Goliath within us. Be Authentically You!

Life is filled with breathtaking moments; minutes you may never experience again, but will leave a lasting impression on you. Take time to pause and experience the fullness in each of those moments. Then live freely in it!

BEHIND THE MAKEUP

FIRST LADY ROSITA "ROSE" GODLOCK
Calvert County Baptist Church
2190 Solomon's Island Rd S
Prince Frederick MD 20678
www.calvertbaptist.org
ligministriesinc@gmail.com
301-780-8382

First Lady Rosita "Rose" Godlock is a native Washingtonian and has resided in Maryland for the past 22 years with her husband Darryl L. Godlock. Reverend Godlock was installed as the Senior Pastor of the Calvert County Baptist Church (CCBC) in August of 2004. The church is located in Prince Frederick MD and is a church plant of the First Baptist Church of Glenarden (FBCG), where Dr. John K. Jenkins, Sr. is the Senior Pastor. Rose accepted Jesus as her Lord and Savior under the ministry of Pastor Jenkins in February 1991. Rose served in various ministries during her 14 years at FBCG including: Women's, Married Couples, Homemakers and Fitness. She served as a facilitator in the Queen Esther Ministry and is a graduate of the Sisters In Discipleship program. Rose has embraced her role as First Lady and enjoys working in ministry alongside her husband in order to further advance the Kingdom of God. She has a passion for women, marriages and cooking! It is her desire to be a vessel God can use to enhance the spiritual journey of those she encounters so that they may experience an abundant life in Christ. Her professional background includes over 20 years in the Financial Industry but she is looking forward to joining her husband in full time ministry. Rose is currently a minister in training under the tutelage of her husband/Pastor and loves studying the scriptures. One of her greatest joys in life has been raising their beautiful daughter Maia (her 'Something Special'). In August 2015 the Godlock's were blessed to gain a son, Westbrook as he took their daughter's hand in marriage. Rose embraces the model of the Proverbs 31 woman and purposes to live a life that is pleasing to God and her husband in order to be an example to women all over world.

SOMETHING SPECIAL

Foundation

I always heard that you don't 'question' God. I usually did okay with that premise until my faith and trust in God were put to the test...several times.

I always wanted a house full of children-like FULL! I would hear people talk about how many kids they desired to have and I could not relate because I wanted as many as I could have. In November of 1992, our beautiful baby girl was born and we named her Maia Simone. She changed my life for the better in so many ways that I never imagined. Lying there as they continued to work on me (she was delivered via C-section); tears flowed uncontrollably as I heard: "It's a girl". Then, more tears flowed as I looked at the most angelic face I had ever seen. Followed by even more tears as I realized she looked just like her FATHER!!! My first thoughts were, Are you kidding me?"...after all I have gone through and she looks like Daddy. Then to make matters worse, she would not look at me. Maia and her daddy had a special bond that was created in the womb as he talked to her, read to her, sang to her, and prayed for her. He loved her and only wanted the best for her from the second he learned of her existence. I could not believe that the moment I had been anticipating was finally here and the only way for her to acknowledge me was to have him stop talking! Once we locked eyes (eventually-lol), it was love at first sight and it continues ever so strong to this day. My Maia Simone is truly a gift from God and I cannot let a day go by without acknowledging how grateful I am for having her in our lives. When I look at her, I see everything that I'm not and more. She has always been her own person, but she is also a mix of her father and me. She has his strength and determination coupled with my wit and charm. She was made by God just for us and I'm so glad He chose us to be her temporary caregivers because truly she belongs to Him!

As wonderful as this new journey was, the enemy didn't want me to have this joy. Many times there was a dark cloud that attempted to overshadow our happiness. There was embarrassment, shame, disappointment, and guilt as we realized that we had disobeyed God. Yes you guessed it...we were not married when Maia was conceived and born. We were saved and loved God, but clearly had not been obedient to His word concerning fornication. We attended a play at church and afterwards there was an altar call and we both rededicated our lives to Christ. As we talked about our experience that evening, we soon found out that we each had made a choice to live holy and that meant that if we were going to stay together then we had to commit to being celibate. We agreed that this was the ONLY way to move forward in our relationship with God and each other. What? Who does that? Can we make it…can we resist the temptation? The answer we found out was a resounding YES! Now don't get me wrong, it was not easy-at all. There were many close calls but we never gave up and we made sure that we had people to hold us accountable. A few months after this play, I found out that I was expecting and she was actually already on the way when we rededicated our lives to Christ that night after the play and I had no idea. For 18 months, we honored our vow to God and each other. We joke now that we barely looked at each other. There was no hugging, kissing, or even hand holding during this time-that's how serious we were! We were married on September 11, 1993 and it was one of the best days of my life. I later realized that by Darryl honoring our commitment to The Lord that he was really demonstrating how much he loved and respected me. We were on the receiving end of what some were calling godly counsel, but it was really condemnation and judgment wrapped in a fake smile. Let me clarify this by saying that we did receive genuine love and support during this time before we were married. There were many, including our Pastor, First Lady, and many in the church and outside of the church that gave us encouragement and helped us in our new roles as young parents and I am forever grateful. Too many times we want to condemn and not restore. We acknowledged our sin and asked God for forgiveness and that was good enough for Him. We did not have anything to prove to man. I have seen people stumble and without the proper guidance and genuine love, they never return to church but more devastating than that is that they never return to God. We serve a forgiving God and He does not want us to live a condemned life. John 3:17 says: "For God did not send His Son into the world to condemn the world, but that the world through Him might be saved". (NKJV).

Eye Shadow

Fast forward to November 1994…a time I will never forget. In October, we found out that baby number two was on the way. We were super duper excited that our family was going to be growing and that Maia would be a big sister. We explained to her (the best way we could to a two –year- old) that Mommy was having a baby. I had been experiencing some pain off and on accompanied by a little spotting, but the Dr. said to take it easy and come in if it did not get better. One morning, I was on my way to take Maia to her childcare provider. I realized that I had forgotten her lunch so we made a quick stop (so I thought) at the grocery store. After being in the store a few moments, I began to feel dizzy and very hot. I asked another shopper if she was hot too and she said no. I proceeded to the aisle to get what I needed and the next thing I felt was the whole store spinning around and in a split second I was on the floor. People rushed to my aid to see if I was okay, but clearly there was something wrong. They put something under my head and tended to me until the paramedics arrived. I was disoriented, scared, and in a lot of pain. I did not know where Maia was, but they reassured me that she was right by my side holding my hand and sitting quietly .The paramedics came and the only thing I could get out was that I was pregnant. They immediately said I was going to the hospital and someone had to come get Maia…faith test number one! I could not reach anyone in the family or a close friend to come and get her. Darryl was working in corrections at the time in Lorton, VA and they could not wait for him to get there. The childcare provider was called, but to my dismay, she could not come because she could not safely drive with the other children across town. I remember saying: "Oh God, help me!" as I laid on the gurney. A woman came over and asked where the sitter lived. It turned out that she lived down the street from the sitter and offered to take Maia to meet her at the corner. In this moment I am in need of emergency medical attention for me and our unborn child then on top of that, I had to trust a complete stranger to take my child! I mustered up enough energy to kiss Maia and pray over her and they whisked me off to the hospital. We later found out that the store manager copied the lady's license and got the babysitter's phone number so they could call to make sure Maia arrived safely…and she did! I heard someone say that you sometimes don't know IF you trust God until you HAVE to trust God…I thought I did but after this, I knew I did! Darryl arrived at the hospital and reassured me that Maia was safe so we now needed to focus on me and the baby. The doctor said that I was miss-carrying the baby. Those words stung like nothing I had ever felt before. My OB/GYN had been alerted of my condition and he instructed us to come to the hospital where he was. That ride seemed to take forever as we left Maryland and went to D.C. Once there, he performed a DNC to 'remove' the fetus. After this painful and traumatic procedure, the Dr. informed me that it did not work and proceeded to do an ultra-sound of my uterus. Shortly thereafter, he told us that I had not had a miscarriage but that it was a tubal pregnancy and I was rushed into surgery. As I was recovering in the hospital, I remember the look of worry and concern on Darryl's face. But the more I stared at him, I began to see something else...he was hurting too! He was being so strong for me, but who was going to be strong for him? I decided right then and there that it had to be me. I asked him how he was and even though he said he was ok, I knew he wasn't. I told him that this was his loss too and I acknowledged that he was hurting and trying to be strong for me. The way he looked at me was a look I had never seen before...God had given us a deeper connection instantly. Oftentimes, the man's feelings in a situation like this are overlooked and they shouldn't be. The men are also grieving and trying to cope with the loss. These challenges do not just affect the woman but I'm not so sure we realize this. From a young age, men are told to be tough, strong, and unemotional. I thank God for giving my husband the courage to feel and share his emotions because it has made him a better husband, father, and friend. In order for us both to heal, we both had to be released to have our moments without being judged by the other person. We needed to be free enough and feel safe enough to trust each other with our hurt. I thank God that He gave that to us, because I'm not sure if we would have survived such a trying time without His grace. With the prayers, love, and support from our families and those close to us (and each other) we started to heal. Before we were even married, we discussed me putting my career on hold to be a full-time homemaker (stay-at-home Mom). Darryl was hesitant to say the least about making this move to live on one income. On Mother's Day 1994, our Pastor's sermon title was, 'The Home Executive.' After hearing this message, Darryl told me to ask my company if I could work part-time so we could prepare for me to come home full-time. Our plan was for me to work until January 1995, then leave the company. Well, sitting in that hospital room, he looked at me and told me to call and ask if I could resign while out on sick leave-they said yes. My big sister typed a letter and so began our journey with me being without any income. Even though we knew I would eventually be home full-time, it was still a little intimidating to think about relying solely on one income. This was no time to waiver in our faith, we had to either believe God or not. We chose to believe Him and totally trust Him to provide for us. Adjusting to being at home with Maia was easy, but thinking about the fact that she would not be a big sister in a few months was no easy task. As the months rolled by and we got closer to the time the baby would've arrived, it was so hard to not focus on what could have been. So many questions in my head: Boy or girl? Who would this baby have looked like? How would Maia have responded to a new baby? What would our lives be like with two small children? And so on and so on. These thoughts consumed me at times so much so that it was hard to focus on anything else and I was just going through the motions of everyday life. There was an underlying numbness that I tried to hide and I believe I got pretty good at hiding it. You see, we learn how to "Talk the talk," "God is good," "I'm blessed and highly favored," and "Our timing is not His timing…" you know the Christian jargon we become able to quote without even thinking. We become masters of "I'm good" when really we are not. I was hurting and it wasn't getting any easier as time went on. I didn't understand this because I was told that time heals all wounds…does it really? I wasn't convinced because while time was truly moving on, my hurting heart was not getting any better. I was so confused and looking for answers that could not be found. I discovered that it was very dangerous to try and keep up this masquerade of, 'it is well with my soul.' I was led to believe that if I expressed my true hurt and disappointment, then that would basically be like insulting my faith in God which I said I had. I didn't understand that I could be free to process and accept my emotions and still honor my love for God and all He had done for me. Somewhere along the way, I began to learn how to slowly balance trusting God, but acknowledging that I was angry. Slowly is not adequate enough to describe this process, but you get the point…it wasn't easy. How do you juggle this emotional roller coaster of being sad regarding your own situation, then rejoicing with others for their good news? I was surrounded by fruitful women to say the least-lol! It seemed as though everywhere I turned, someone was having a baby or two…or three! There was excitement in the air, but it was also hard for me to embrace it. I know for a fact that I was not the only one suffering from a loss, but it sure can feel that way. It is very dangerous to think that you are the ONLY one going through a trial. The enemy wants to isolate you and convince you that you are in this thing alone. I am grateful for sound biblical teaching, because without it, I truly believe I could've lost my mind. Now don't get me wrong, it was hard to be genuinely excited for others having babies when I wanted another so badly. I did not want to be phony, so I had to ask God to help me be genuine in my expression of joy towards others when their family was growing. I was supported by girlfriends that acknowledged my hurt and handled me gingerly during this time and I am still grateful for them today. The world we live in can be cold and people can be selfish, but God wants us to be feeling caring and self-less. We cannot only focus on our little world. There are people right under our noses that are silently suffering and if we are not careful, they will slip under the radar. If you sense that something is not right, then it usually isn't, but you have to use wisdom and discernment in your approach. The best thing to do first is to ask God if you are the one He wants to use in the situation. I never want to force myself upon someone, but I also don't want to miss what God may be trying to accomplish by not being in tune with hearing His voice. We are oftentimes just called to pray even when we have insight or first-hand knowledge of what someone is going through. God can use anyone He chooses to speak life into a dead situation, but it may not be you. You may just be the one called to stand in the gap and intercede on their behalf because maybe they don't even have the strength to pray anymore. Trust me, I have been in that place where I didn't even know where to begin when it was time to talk to God. Yes, He knows my heart, but I needed words and didn't have them. I know beyond a shadow of a doubt that others were standing in the gap for me and I am eternally thankful. Now, it is the least I can do for someone else. I learned first-hand how important it is to have strong women in your life to help you in this journey. So let me encourage you to take the super-hero cape off and come out of the phone booth…you are not Wonder Woman and you cannot do this alone!

Fast forward to November 1996…I suspected that something was going on and decided to take a pregnancy test. It was positive so I told hubby and called the Dr. Since I was still under the care of the same OB/GYN, he was excited, but cautious. I was scheduled to come in for blood work and a sonogram as soon as possible. I think I could've bitten my nails clean off during this time! Here we go again with the emotional roller coaster. We were excited about the baby… nervous about the tests. Oh no! God I don't want to doubt you, but I'm so scared. What will the results be? So we did the only thing we knew how to do-pray and move forward with the appointment. The blood work was positive, but the sonogram revealed another tubal pregnancy so off to another surgery then on to processing the feelings from almost exactly two years prior all over again. We were devastated to say the least. Not again!! I wanted so badly to be strong, but it was very difficult. We had not told many people this time around (including the now four- year -old Maia). Not having to share the news outside of our inner circle that once again our baby did not make it was somewhat better, but it was hard nonetheless to tell even a few. I didn't want to see another sad face when others found out because every time I looked in the mirror there was a sad face staring right back at me. Many days I didn't even want to look in the mirror because I didn't want to see 'her.' The real me was full of life and vitality, but this new person, I didn't like her…she had no joy, no ambition and, I did not enjoy being around her. But I couldn't escape her presence because we were one in the same. Each day was a struggle to find myself and find the joy I once knew. I promise you I struggled with not asking God why because it was something that I thought was off limits. How dare I question the Almighty Himself? He was the maker of all things and who was I to question Him and doubt His ability to know what's best for me? What right did I think I had to come face to face with a God who is all-knowing? How could I not be grateful that we had a gifted, smart, funny and precious little girl already? I'm glad you asked! I was so focused on my dream of having a house full of children that I could not see the beauty of being the mother of an awesome kid. I really did believe I was grateful for her, but I wasn't because every chance I got I would dwell on the two that we didn't have. Shortly after the first loss, I went to church because there was just something about hearing my pastor preach that soothed my spirit. I always felt that God was speaking directly to me and no one else when I sat under his teaching and preaching. After service he saw me and asked why I was back so soon after going through the loss of the baby. I told him that I just had to be there. I was in so much pain (emotionally and physically) but just being in the house of God made me feel better. We walked down the hallway so I could wait for Darryl to get the car and he told me that everything would be ok and that God had something special for me. I really wanted to believe him, but in that moment I couldn't. Two years later, I couldn't help but wonder how God could have something special for me now and not when those two precious babies were wanted so badly. How much more could He have for me than the two babies I would never hold? I wanted to be positive and hopeful and to some degree deep down inside I think my spirit knew He was telling the truth. I just had to wait for my mind to catch up and that was the hard part. Have you ever felt like you were literally in two places at the same time? Pray don't pray…trust God don't trust God…smile don't smile…and on it goes. Well that's where I was. I didn't know if I was coming or going. Even though I was close to Darryl and he had been with me every step of the way so far, there was another issue that no one warned me about. In these four years and after two failed pregnancies, I was distant when it came to sex. In my mind if we couldn't make a baby then, I didn't want to have sex. Dealing with infertility is multi-faceted. There are so many dynamics that most people wouldn't even think about especially if you have not walked down that road. By now we knew that it would not be possible to conceive because while I did have one ovary, I had lost both fallopian tubes with the tubal pregnancies. The only options for us to conceive were In Vitro Fertilization or adoption, and we could not agree on which route to take nor could we afford either option. So yet again we were faced with more emotional challenges to deal with on top of the normal ups and downs in life. Many conversations were had and many prayers were prayed. Every now and then I would start a conversation about adoption, but to no avail. It was just not meant to be and I had to accept it. For an adult, accepting life's challenges is hard, but, try explaining some of these challenges to a young child. As Maia got older, she started to ask why she didn't have a sister or brother. Whew! This was hard because most of the families we spent time with had more than one child so she wondered why she didn't have any siblings. We would tell her that we had to ask God for a sister or brother. She would pray and ask for a sibling, then as she got older she would leave us notes asking for one. Now, in addition to dealing with our own emotions, we had to help Maia deal with hers. Harder than accepting the fact that our family would not be growing was watching her try to process this as a child. One of the most heart-breaking moments came when she asked why God wouldn't give us a baby. How do you answer that? While I don't remember the exact answer, I can recall feeling hopeless and lost for words. As she grew older, she found a way to accept it as we had, but it was definitely a struggle and she did not give up easily when it came to asking. As she spent time with larger families, it became apparent that being an only child had its benefits. There were no issues with sharing us or her things with anyone else and over time she learned to deal with it and eventually accepted it. Early on, I mentioned having feelings of guilt when I was an unwed expectant young adult. As our challenges with having more children came over the years, the guilt returned. I not only felt guilty for not giving Maia a sibling, but I also felt guilty for not being able to give Darryl more children. I especially struggled with him not having a son because I knew he would've been great with a son. He was a fantastic father to Maia and I have no doubt that he would have been just as great with a boy.

Lipstick

When you are faced with a situation that you absolutely cannot change, there has to be a moment when you come to grips with your reality and move forward. I know you are wondering how I did this. Well strangely enough, I didn't get my release or breakthrough until I was honest with God. The reason this was strange to me in that time is because I knew God had full understanding of what was in my heart. So how could I be honest with Him? One day, as I was lying in the bed, a flood of emotions came over me and the next thing I know, I am in a full out temper tantrum (for lack of better words) like a toddler wanting a cookie. I had been holding on to feelings of hurt, shame, disappointment, and anger and I couldn't hold it in any longer. I let it all go and I told God exactly how I felt. I asked Him why me? I expressed my frustration with not being able to have more children and feeling inadequate as a woman and a wife. I told God that it wasn't fair and last but not least, I told God that I was mad at Him! I know you're probably thinking that I must have lost my mind to behave this way with the very One that gave me life. But what you may not understand (because I sure didn't) is that in order for me to heal, I had to release those emotions. I could no longer walk around living a lie. I was going about life as if all was well, but it wasn't. I was bitter and God could not be to me who I needed Him to be as long as I was harboring bitterness. It was not possible for me to truly be free in Christ and have ill feelings toward Him at the same time. I don't have to remember the exact date and time, but I do remember as if it were yesterday the relief I felt. I know beyond the shadow of a doubt that had it not been for this release, I would not have been able to heal. There is no way I could grow closer to Jesus and those around me without being free. While it may seem unorthodox to some, trust me I know that for me this is what had to happen...it was necessary for me. I can't speak for anyone else, but I can tell you that I changed that very day. I was all alone in the room, but I know The Lord was with me and He heard my cries. There were tears that flowed that day like I had never experienced before and I literally didn't think I had any left when it was all said and done. There is no way we could experience the wonderful marriage and family life we have had without my breakthrough. If someone had told me that is what I would have to go through, I'm pretty sure I would think they were crazy. When it was all said and done, God said to me: "That's all I wanted you to do was to be honest with yourself because I already knew how you felt...now you have received your healing." It is because of this moment that I was able to share my testimony with other women and even couples experiencing the hurt and pain of infertility. Had I not experienced this moment with God, I would not have been able to enjoy raising such a phenomenal daughter. Everything that we sacrificed over the years was all worth it to see her grow into an awesome young woman. I often joked about feeling like I was the mother of many children because of her many moods and maybe that was God giving me a taste of what I was missing. Eventually, I came to a place where I appreciated just having one, especially when it came to providing. Kids are expensive and my hat goes off to families with multiple children. I was very blessed over the years at home to provide childcare for several families and I thank God and the parents for trusting me with their precious children. We also have been chosen to be the godparents of 11 children and I am forever grateful for each and every one of them. None of this would have been possible if I had not been delivered from the anger and bitterness I was holding on to all of those years. When I think of how much I could have missed out on, I can't help but rejoice. I know I'm not the only one who has experienced a traumatic loss in one form or another. I also know that I'm not the only one that almost gave up on God. What are you holding on to? What do you need to release? What is your 'Something Special' that you could be missing out on? A career opportunity, a healthy marriage, being a parent, sister, friend, mentor, a ministry calling, starting your own business; etc...Don't focus on what you don't have in your life. I challenge you to focus on what you DO have...because God has 'Something Special' in store for you too!

First Lady Tamika I. Parran
eChurch (Everybody's Church)
1907 Columbia Ave
Landover, MD 20785
TamikaParran@hotmail.com
(301) 801-0478

Tamika Parran, First Lady of eChurch, is the eldest daughter of Dr. Lawrence and Elder Jean Jointer. In her formative years, she attended the Mobile Ministries church, where she gave her heart to the Lord and gained a solid foundation of God's Word under the leadership by Bishop Bette E. Funn.

First Lady Tamika is a woman of faith and lives out Proverbs 31 as a virtuous woman. As a wife, she lovingly supports her husband, Pastor Damon Parran in his God-given vision for eChurch and for their personal and professional lives. They married in November, 1998 and have three lovely daughters, Rayne, Skyla and Soleil.

As First Lady of eChurch, she has a passion for worship and is committed to spiritual and educational excellence. She is a gifted praise team leader. She is also the founder of the Victorious Ladies of Purpose, a monthly bible study for women, now celebrating its 10th year. She is a powerful teacher of the gospel and rightly divides the Word of truth. She has a heart for mothers and children issues.

She has an undergraduate degree in Education from Bowie State University and Masters degrees in Administration and Curriculum Instruction from McDaniel College.

First Lady is committed to worshipping God in every facet of her being. While she wears many hats, she has the God-given ability to wear them all well.

CONFIDENCE COURSE
Girl Triumphant

How can I say thanks, for the things you have done for me, things so undeserved that you gave to prove your love for me, the voices of a million angels could not express my gratitude. All that I am and ever hope to be, I owe it all to thee. Thank you Fanny Crosby, for those song lyrics that express my feelings exactly.

I am so grateful for all the Lord has done in my life. For how far He has brought me and for the distance He has promised to take me.

Foundation:

My story is one of triumph. Triumph over the tumultuous trap called Comparison. Theodore Roosevelt once said, "Comparison is the thief of joy." You see, I grew up the oldest of three children; my mother, a teacher, and my father, for most of my life, a principal. From a very young age, I was told that I could be and do anything, and that even the sky was not the limit. My father taught me valuable lessons about being a person of my word and that integrity was everything! My mother made sure that we stayed in church, Bible study, prayer meetings, revivals, and all conferences. I am extremely grateful for that. Not to mention the litany of hymnals. I now know because of that. Our house was one of love, one where we would play church and have "communion" almost nightly. The best part was when we would sing, At Calvary," and only get to the second verse before we would all break out in a shout. Good Times.

Having such a strong Foundation made confidence come quite easy for me. As I moved through high school playing on the volleyball team, being captain of the cheerleading squad, and later leading praise and worship as a teenager, leadership roles were not scary or thought of as a daunting task to be undertaken, yet something that I lounged freely into as I saw the opportunity arise. I had been raised to never look down on myself or others for that matter. This led me to be kind and caring towards others and to speak life into all those whom I came in contact with, it was a way of life, a lesson taught to me by my mother. Not so much in what she said, but by the way she carried herself and lived her life in front of us.

Little did I know that my upbringing was preparing me for my position as First Lady. (Now, many people have their own names for the pastors' wife, such as Lady, or Only Lady; however, this one works for us, so that is what we use.) This position well…is it really a position, or is it a calling? Perhaps a ministry of its own? I say all three, perhaps. By definition, a position is a place where someone or something is located or has been put; a location, situation, spot, site, locality, setting, or area.

This is where I am, my spot, my setting, my area. I embrace it.

When my husband became Pastor I was assigned to this position, although I didn't apply for it, it became mine. My husband was handed this pastoral mantel by his grandfather at the age of twenty-four. We had only been married for two years, when he was installed. Weeks before this, my husband was asked this question by another Pastor, "Is your wife ready to be a First Lady?" Initially, I was highly offended. This man knew me. Didn't he think I was nice and sweet? Didn't he think that I would be able to work well with others? Didn't he think I could make a mean tuna salad for the potluck? Didn't he think I would look good in a big hat? Yet, after some time had passed, I understood the weightiness of the question. It had nothing to do with smiles, potlucks, and big hats, and I was ready with the answer to that question. It was… I think so.

What is a calling? The dictionary says: a calling is a strong urge toward a particular way of life or career, a profession, an occupation, a call.

Is this a calling? For me, not quite an occupation even though a lot of work is involved. Hey, if this is an occupation, did my paycheck get lost in the mail? (Note to self: contact post office.)

I digress. Yes, defiantly a call though. You have to be called to be in this role, no doubt. So keeping with that, yes there is a strong pull or urge to do the Will of Christ and to be the best that you can be. Then we ask: Is it ministry? Let's stick a pin in that, I promise, we will come back to that one later.

Being so young, starting out as First Lady, I found myself in a strange place. This place was odd…it was different and extremely scary. For the first time in my life, I was unsure. I was questioning myself and doubting everything. You see I had big shoes to fill. My husband's grandmother had been the former first lady for over 30 years.

Who was I? How was I going to ever be like her? Why did I think I had to be? She was wonderful in her own right. I wanted to be wonderful, too. I didn't want to fail at this…come on, who wants to fail at anything? But failing at this would mean that I would be letting people down, a lot of people and in my mind, the Lord too. I didn't want to fail Him or displease the Lord with my actions or lack thereof.

I had grown up in a church where there was a female pastor, and although she taught us the Word in all its fullness, I didn't know quite what a first lady was supposed to do or be because I had not grown up with one. I began to do some homework on the subject. I began to look closely and take notes on the ladies in that position, as we would visit other churches. Makes sense though, right? If you want to know about something, you research it. I'm not saying that I sat with pen, notepads, whiteout, and a recording device. No, I watched and studied from afar, watching to see how these ladies walked and talked and dressed.

Sidebar: Why is it that most of them could play the piano? Well, there goes that!

So the study begins…

Case study#1- There was First Lady Annette, who was so very kind and sweet to all of the members and visitors; greeting everyone with a smile, a hug, and a, "Isn't God good?" She was joyful and her laugh was infectious. But no sooner than the laugh had cleared the air like vapor; she would turn around and disrespect her husband openly. Saying things like, "What are you talking about?" and "That makes no sense," or "What are you thinking?" The statements were loud and the tone was chilling.

I didn't want to be like her.

So on to the next one…

Case study #2- Then there was First Lady Bethany, she could preach heaven down, as they say, and pray until you felt your pew shake. Yes, she was fire all by herself! Her messages were powerful and when people knew she was taking the stage, they would sit up straight and tall, careful not to miss one word. But then…I saw another side, the side that needed to "run" the church, the side that was attempting to snatch headship from her husband because she could "do it better" (she had been told that many times I'm sure) and the side that was in everything and everywhere… but in the Will of God.

God would be displeased if I were like her.

So on to the next one…

Case study #3- Lastly, there was First Lady Casey, very giving and a true servant. She had a quiet nature and you rarely knew she was in the room. I wish I could tell you more about her…but she had nothing to say. Nothing. About anything. No opinion. Nope. None. At all. Just sat and smiled, all of the time… Ok.

I couldn't be like her… So what was I to do?

I had done my homework trying to gauge this role and see it in a better light. Now normally I am a proponent of homework, but in this case it was a bad idea. I had done my due diligence and studied and gathered all of my data and I was back to square one. Confusion. Who was I to be?

Now let me say this, I now see that there were first ladies that were in their roles and pleasing God as they lived it out. However, I believe that the Lord allowed me not to see all of the great things that were to be seen so that I could ultimately find my way to Him and seek direction. He was the one who wanted to construct this project. He wanted to develop this lump of clay. If I had honed in on all of the great examples around me I would have turned into a mirror image of those I had seen. This never would have caused me joy or any type of fulfillment. Our God is so wise; He knows what is best for us.

You see when you are used to always navigating your own path and really never experience intimidation; this place…this place of uncertainty is quite disheartening. I wanted to know where I fit in, in this ministry. I had never had to fit in before or find my place. Now I was walking in shoes I felt were three sizes too big. I didn't look like anyone else. I wanted to know, what I was supposed to do or be. So maybe I would wear a big hat.

Maybe I would were suits every Sunday. No, that wasn't me.

I just recently cleaned out one of my closets and it was filled with suits that were classified as "first lady" suits. What was I thinking, dressing like I was way older than I was? Honestly, I was not trying to impress anyone; I just thought that was what I was supposed to do and how I was supposed to look. I still felt like I didn't fit the mold. THE mold. What mold? I wish I knew then that only God creates and fashions us, not man.

The love I felt from our church family during that time was overwhelming. They surrounded me with such love and embraced me with such openness. It wasn't them, it was me. It was all me, my un-assuredness, my own self-conscious, my own ever-present state of confusion. I didn't want to let them down. I didn't want to let my husband down.

Comparing is such a dangerous action. Rick Warren, author of the *Purpose Driven Life* once said, "When you strive to be the person God made you to be, you'll find real meaning, purpose, fulfillment, and satisfaction. You can't focus on *your* purpose while looking at other people." At that point in my life I hadn't realized this revelation. All I had to do was strive to be who God wanted and created me to be. There I would find satisfaction. I had spent a great deal of time feeling unsatisfied.

By all means, we should have role models and people that we look up to and admire. However, we must realize that there is a thin line between comparing yourself to someone and admiring someone. When you admire a person, you look at them and see ways in which you would like to be better, do better, or live life better. The way you see them inspires you to do greater things. You do this with ambition, purpose, and zeal. We all should have people in our lives that we admire for all of the personal benefits that come with pure admiration.

However, when you compare yourself to someone you begin to find fault in where you are or what you have. You may have been at an event where you looked around and saw how others were dressed and felt less than or inferior. Maybe not even an event but just on a regular day. Maybe your hair was not as nice or as stylish as it could have been, maybe your car was an older model compared to the people in your circle. What a horrible feeling it is to compare yourself to another. You feel it in the pit of your stomach and it leaves a bitter taste in your mouth not to mention the frustration that can lead to envy, strife, and sadness.

At this time, I was starting to wish that I was like other first ladies that I had seen.

Alright, I'll say it, I became quite jealous. Jealous of those that had special reserved seating, adjutants, or even those that could sit and support their husbands without leaving the service to tend to a crying child or change a diaper. I became intimidated, more feelings of frustrated. The devil was playing a real head game with me and I was the perfect opponent, the kind that didn't fight back. The kind that just sat down as if a defeated foe. I regret the fact that I actually would get mad at my husband, strictly based on my own insecurities and unspoken wishes. I wasn't like everyone else, and that wasn't a bad thing. I was me and that was a great thing. It just took me a while to see that.

This was a real spirit of distraction. This spirit had me comparing myself to everyone around me, worrying that I wasn't good enough and thinking that I was not living up to the imaginary bar that I had set. Because of this, I lost sight of some of the most important things in life. Like being present, living in the moment, enjoying life, and enjoying family. Being happy. Finding joy. Praising God. If the devil can get us distracted with things like jobs, problems, family, friends, boyfriends, and girlfriends he wins. He wins because we have taken our eyes off of God and have let the cares of this life momentarily shift us. We have all done it, once we realize what we have done we must repent and move forward, no need to look back. We say Lord we are sorry that we saw the bigness of our situation and not the bigness of our God.

I was asked to attend a women's conference, about ten years ago, and I reluctantly went, mainly because I wouldn't know anyone there except for the person who had invited me. And since she was part of the conference, I knew I probably would not see much of her. Which I didn't. Anyway, there was a lunch break in the schedule, which I was not looking forward to, as I knew I would have to find someone to eat with. Awkward, well for me anyway. So as I walked around looking for somewhere to sit, I found a table with two ladies that I had seen before at other functions so I gladly joined them, and three other ladies later completed our table.

Everything was going well, we were all first ladies, they would start in on a topic and I would chime in every now and again. Everyone at this table was at least thirty-five years my senior, but we were laughing and enjoying our food as equals.

After a while, the tone of the conversation turned serious and we began to discuss a TV evangelist recently on the news, I again chimed in as everyone else did, but this time was shut down in the middle of my sentence. One of the women at the table, began to tell me that I was wrong in my view of the situation and loudly yelled, "Are you listening to me, are – you- listening to -me?" While staring closely into my face and rising from her chair, I replied to her, " Yes, ma'am I hear you." Which was a play on words because I was not listening, I did hear her though, and so did everyone else there, but I was not about to disrespect someone who could have easily been my grandmother.

No one at the table said a word. My heart was broken.

I thought I was fitting in with these ladies, at least for lunch. Yet, I was yelled at and treated like an insignificant peasant or as if I was a child who needed to be reprimanded for speaking out of turn. I wanted to cry, but not at *that* table. Never that. I sat for a few more minutes and choked down some cake, then excused myself to the bathroom. I cried. First Lady Blah Blah was so rude, so loud, for no reason. I wasn't crying because of what she said. It was more about the feeling that yet again I didn't fit.

As I was getting myself together in the bathroom in order to return to the table, one of the first ladies who was also the main speaker for the occasion came in, she was a well-dressed, sharp looking lady maybe seventy-years-old or so. She came in and put her arm around me, she told me that she had seen and heard what happened and also how I had responded. She then replied, "You are one classy lady." Wow. Those words were like healing waters to my broken spirit. I looked into her eyes, tears still flowing and said, "Thank you for that."

I learned a lesson, a lesson that God would fight my battles. That I didn't then, nor do I now, have to rely on my own strength to war against Satan. There will be times when we will have to verbally stand our ground and make our voices and opinions heard. We were never created to be anyone's doormat. But on that day, God was showing me something, He was opening my eyes to the fact that He had my back. He showed me then, that even when I don't know what to say, He will give me what to say and sometimes…it's nothing at all.

Eye Shadow:

Not long after that, I was sitting on the front row of church after service wearing a slightly tilted halo of confusion; the Lord said to me "Who have I made you to be?" It dropped in my spirit just as clear as day. I had never sought the Lord to give me direction as to who I was to be, who He was making me to be, and how I was to operate in this role. I had just been taking copious notes and watching a lot of people, but never lifted the question to the Lord. No wonder I felt like the children on Israel wondering around in what was my own personal wilderness. How do we ever think that we can navigate this life with all that it brings without seeking the face of God? Why did I think I would ever find what I was looking for with out consulting the Lord? So that is where the light at the end of the tunnel began to become evident.

I prayed this prayer:

Dear Lord, I come to you in no strength of my own, asking you for your guidance. I have been in this role of first lady and I don't feel like I have anything to offer. I feel confused and I feel alone. Help me to see your Will for my life, help me to hear your voice. I don't want to be a carbon copy of anyone or a poor imitation of another. Help me to be the best me, I can be. Amen.

I'm sure that there was more to the prayer, but these are the lines that I found myself repeating on more than one occasion, so I know them pretty much by heart. It seems that when you are staying before the Lord about something you seem to pray the same prayer over and over again. Sometimes your heart just finds a few words to express how you feel. Other times no words can be found, and it is in those times that we rejoice in knowing that our God can hear our hearts and prayers, even when we can't verbalize them.

When you have been in a state of confusion, the devil plays tricks on your mind, like making you feel that you are alone. No, at the time I didn't have a lot of friends that were around my age that also were pastors' wives, but I was never alone. That was a trick of the enemy, and I had to become quite vigilant in warding off these tricks. I had learned to pray even as a child by using the words, Devil we are not ignorant of your devises! How powerful is that! Serving notice on the enemy. Yes Indeed. The devil will have you doubting everything that you have been taught and most of what you know to be true.

Proverbs 3:26 says; For the Lord will be your confidence, and will keep your foot from being caught. We as women seem to compare ourselves to each other far to often.

When the Lord formed us, He formed us in His image, He knew us before our own mothers did. The word says in Jeremiah 1:5; Before I formed thee in the belly I knew thee; and before thou camest forth out of the womb I sanctified thee. He makes no mistakes, but the best part of it all is that He doesn't make carbon copies. Thank you God, for revealing this to me.

Lipstick

Great, so now things are looking up and brighter days were ahead…well almost…I still had to seek the Lord about ministry. Ministry…Yes, this is a ministry. Mine is three-fold. The Lord told me to take care of our children, which is a very important part of ministry as pastor's children go through spiritual attacks as well. He also told me that I was to minister to my husband, as no one can intercede for him like I can.

Proverbs 31: 26-28 says; She opened her mouth with wisdom; and in her tongue is the law of kindness. She looketh well to the ways of her household, and eateth not the bread of idleness. Her children arise up, and call her blessed; her husband also, and he praiseth her.

Best of all once I gave it all over to the Lord and really spent time in prayer and in His Word He began to unfold what MY ministry was, not just the role that I played in THE ministry. Indeed I was going to take good care of our three daughters, I pride myself on that. Like I mentioned before, they go through attacks as well. If the devil can't get to the man of God, he attacks those closest to him. They live under a magnifying glass;

people watch them as if they are exempt from life because their father is a preacher. It is because I understand that, that I cover my children in prayer, I ask the Lord to be a fence all around them. I can't always be there, but our God is omnipotent, omnipresent and omniscient.

And make no doubt about it, I was going to take care of my husband and make sure that he was always prepared to minister and that I was, as Dr. Phil says, his "soft place to fall." God just gave me a deeper insight into how important this ministry was, and how I could not allow my areas of insecurities to dictate the relationship that I would have with my husband. I was being a hindrance at times instead of being a help. No, I was not being rude or talking down to him, but I was more focused on me and finding out who I was to be in this role, to really be the strong support system that I could have been. I was too distracted to be the prayer warrior I should have been for him. Admittedly, sidetracked and could not see the bigger picture. And that picture was, *Us Against the World.* I know better now.

Yet, this still leads me to MY ministry, you see I am a teacher at heart, so the Lord confirmed what I already was starting to feel in my spirit and that was that He would use me to teach the gospel. The Lord gave me the women's ministry with the title Victorious Ladies of Purpose; this ministry has been a blessing to me as well as other women. However, my ministry also includes the ministry of praise and worship. Since I was a pre-teen, I have been leading songs in church. Being young, you lead the congregation in songs that you like and those that get people on their feet. But as you grow in Christ and build a stronger relationship with Him, you understand that praise and worship is very different and that what you are doing, albeit exciting, is also ministry. I love how each Sunday I have the opportunity to look out over the church and see hands raised and eyes closed as people actively join in song and surrender, making a connection to God. I am so blessed that I have the ability to be a part of it all.

Many people will put titles or positions on you that God never gave to you. But when you know what God told you, you are unmoved by what people say or think. When you have this assurance, you begin to move out in your gift and calling without fear or reserve.

After my second daughter was born and while on maternity leave, I began to write poetry, nothing-fancy just thoughts that came into my head. I wrote this one after I began to feel more positive about the journey that I was on and more excited about where it would lead.

Go

Go be bold and wonderful,

Go be joyful and dance,

Go be peaceful and vigilant,

Go be fearless and strong,

Go stand tall and still,

Go pray and listen,

Go seek and find,

Go witness and change the world,

Go.

With Christ on my side and in my life I am free to live an authentic life. One where He walks and talks with me and I am not only able to do the same, but I am able to gain true insight and fresh revelation. Having a relationship with Christ is the key. You can go to church every Sunday and every Wednesday night for Bible study, but if you don't have a relationship with Christ you are missing out. You can't have a successful marriage if you never spend time with the person or speak to the person and allow the person to speak to you. You may have a marriage on paper, but there is no true relationship. This close bond with Christ will enable you to see clearly His will for you and allow you to walk out on faith. Faith and Fear cannot occupy the same space. Fear will immobilize us. My husband, Pastor Damon, preached once, that fear is the calling card of Satan and that we must reject fear and embrace faith!

Another thing that I learned is that having a strong prayer life is paramount. No matter what your job or title is, prayer is essential. Because I had a minimal prayer life, I was weak in some areas leaving myself open to discouragement. Remember that closet that I cleaned out with all the items that I thought made me look the part? Well in the empty cedar closet I have now created a battle room. Yes, battle (wink). A room that is just for praying. When you understand that spiritually our weapons of warfare are not carnal, meaning that they cannot be felt or seen, you grasp the concept that you battle on your knees.

Growing up, we would have all night prayer and the children would be a part of it too. We would have it at our Pastor's home and she would kindly set up a roll away bed because she knew we would try to pray from 10pm to 6am like the adults did, but that never happened. We tried. We don't hear about all night prayer meetings that much anymore. However, the need for prayer has remained the same, if not more so now than ever.

For too long, we have lived our lives trying to be like someone else. Trying to preach, pray, teach, or even dress like someone that we have seen on television or in real life. When we do that, we are telling the Lord that what He made wasn't good enough. But it was. I am. You are. We are.

The Word says in Psalms 139:14; I will praise You, for I am fearfully *and* wonderfully made; marvelous are Your works, and *that* my soul knows very well.

Practice speaking life over yourself daily. As you know, life and death are in the power of the tongue, so choose Life!

These are 10 affirmations that I have created in order to encourage myself in the Lord daily and to remind myself who I am and whose I am.

~My God says, I am fearfully and wonderfully made.

He makes no mistakes, so look in the mirror and love what you see. You are a work of art.

~My God made me the head and not the tail.

We have everything we need to be overcomers. We have the Word so we always win.

~My God shall supply all of my needs.

Whatever I stand in need of, my God will provide. He knows what I need.

~My God is a very present help in the time of trouble.

When troubles arise, He will be our shield. We don't have to worry.

~My God will never leave me or forsake me.

Even when you don't see anyone around, you are not alone. He will remember you.

~My God will fight battles and go to war for me.

I don't have to fight. He will do that for me. I will sit and watch.

~My God will heal all of my sicknesses and disease.

He will make my body whole. He will cure all infirmities.

~My God allows me to walk in authority.

I walk with my head held high. I have power over all of my enemies.

~My God loves me.

No one loves my more that He does. I belong to Him.

~My God is my peace.

The peace that He gives to me, the world can't recreate it. The world can't take it away.

    I truly am who God says I am; He never said that I was not enough. He never said that I was not strong or intelligent. Those were lies from the devil, which I not only listened to but also allowed myself to believe. My God never meant for me to compare myself with anyone or to measure my success by someone else's. We quote the scriptures that we are beautifully and wonderfully made but do we really believe that? Or maybe we believe that some of the time, those times when all is right with the world. Of course, it is easy to smile during that time and sing the song by Bette Midler, "Everything's coming up roses."

Lets face it, we don't always feel confident, but those are the times that we have to rebuke the devil as he is trying to steal our joy. We must realize and remind ourselves that it is the devil that comes to steal, kill, and destroy, but Christ has come to give us life and that life more abundantly. I have gotten to a point in my life that I refuse to look down on myself. It was a long process, one that started with one step, a step that led me to ask God what He wanted from my life and how He wanted me to operate in it. We find ourselves in a place of unrest when we look at others and how other people live their lives and we began to compare. Not being content in where we are, or how God made us. You don't have to stay in a place where you are unhappy, but while you are there, and praying for growth, change, or a different outlook, don't fall into depression or sadness. However, in this state praise Him in advance for what you know He will do. I heard a quote once that said, "While you are waiting for God to open a door, praise Him in the hallway. I love that. I had to wait on the Lord and pray. Wait for Him to show me where I had come up short and where I needed to make changes, because if the truth were told, we all need some readjustments. Once I began to work on me, the Lord began to show me where I should focus my time and efforts and the areas in which He would use me to make a difference. Going through this process gave me a sense of peace. I am at peace with me. Thank God for peace.

The voices of a million angels could not express my gratitude, for all that the Lord has taught me. He has opened my eyes to so many things. I am now a strong, assured woman of God, one who knows her calling and is excited about her destiny. That said, I'm not immune to the darts that the enemy throws; however, I now know that I have the tools in order to block them. It took some time to get to this place, but like a butterfly emerging from the cocoon, our God makes all things beautiful in His time. I pray that my story encourages you to move forward in the path that God has for you and that it inspires you to be your absolute best, comparing yourself to no one but your past self, constantly trying to be better. As my testimony comes to a close, I leave you with this Word from Galatians 6:4, "Let everyone be sure to do his very best, for then he will have the personal satisfaction of work done well and won't need to compare himself with someone else." Peace be with you.

BEHIND THE MAKEUP

Pastor Tiffany Bryan
Greater Lighthouse Church
5201 Baltimore Lane
Lanham, MD 20706
LadytBryan34@gmail.com
(301) 306-4420

Co-Pastor Tiffany Bryan was born on March 26th to Emma L. Davis and the late John W. Fielding. She is a native of Prince George's County, Maryland where she received her primary education. She has been married to Pastor Joseph D. Bryan for nineteen years and is the proud mother of three wonderful children; Doneze, Jacqael and John. Her love is for serving her family, her church, and her community. Co-Pastor Tiffany Bryan is a twenty year employee, currently serving as a Human Resource Specialist within the U.S. Government, in which she has the opportunity to support those at the highest levels of Government.

In 1998 she was granted the opportunity to serve on the Board of Elders and on the intercessory team at the National Prayer Chapel in which she received her indoctrination into ministry. Co-Pastor Tiffany accepted the call alongside her husband, Pastor Joseph D. Bryan, in 2000 in founding Jesus Christ Church of Temple Hills. During her seven year tenure she served as the Women's Ministry president and youth advisor. In 2008, Co-Pastor Tiffany Bryan transitioned alongside her husband Pastor Bryan to preside as Pastors of the Greater Lighthouse Church, where they now serve under the leadership of Apostle Joseph W. Bryan and Evangelist Pearl V. Bryan, D.D. She continues to serve as the Women's Ministry President, Marriage Enrichment Facilitator, Music Department Director, Ministry Wives Group Founder and President, and Executive Advisor on the Board of Elders.

Co-Pastor Tiffany Bryan's greatest passion is to empower women to walk in the light of God's love; to see families restored, and marriages healed.

OUR LEADING LADY
Run Away Bride

Foundation

I'd married young and had already had a beautiful baby boy six months prior to our wedding ceremony. My life had drastically changed, seemed like overnight. I'd finally escaped into my own world of independence. I could make my own decisions now without hearing anyone else's opinion about what I should or shouldn't do. What a point of freedom….so I thought. I soon learned that with freedom comes a great deal of responsibility. Was I really ready?

Now at 19 years of age I had to care for a baby boy, a husband, and manage my own home. I'd never had to do these things before. All of my young life, I'd never had the opportunity to take care of anyone beyond me; and surely, that task was very minimal. I was raised in a home where my parents practically did everything for us, with an exception to some cleaning, of course. So it was all really brand new. As time went on, in my beautiful world of independence, I began to experience what I'd like to call the shock of life. There was no one there to help me figure it all out. At least that's what I told myself. It seemed like everyone was against the fact that I was marrying so young; but I was so in love that I made up in my mind that I was going to do it and then all would be proven wrong. I can do this I thought, but sooner rather than later, the inevitable happened, and our honeymoon stage soon dwindled down to the mundane every day come and go. Some days it seemed as if we were passing each other without any real conversation. I will admit, it was ok with me because I would be so exhausted after a long day at work. I just wanted to sleep.

It was crazy, my emotions were everywhere. With each passing day it felt like I was sinking deeper and deeper into depression. I can only imagine how my husband was feeling as he had to deal with my continued decline of happiness. I found myself crying at times for no reason. What was happening to me? Was I losing it? Who would I talk to, besides I'd tried so hard to prove that I could handle things on my own, and letting it out to my closest friends and family would mean that I was a failure. No one could know really what I was feeling inside. My pillow became my escape and my eyelids longed to shut as I would somehow retreat into dreamland. Sleep and more sleep is what I did. I'd lost my passion for love; I'd lost my passion for life.

As more time passed, I'd learned to push through these emotions enough to continue my daily routine of going to work, coming home, doing a little house work, caring for our son, and attending church often. By this time, I'd picked up a passion for the Word of God. Every day, I'd read and read. It was as if the words were jumping off of the pages at me. It made me feel better somehow. One morning, as I was turning the television to watch the news, I happened to land on a channel where Joyce Meyers was teaching. I can't remember now what it was she was teaching about, but somehow her words began to lift my heart and I found strength to keep moving. I began to really develop a passion for praying and seeking God. It was like a new found love. At every turn, and at every free moment, I'd read the Word. As soon as I hit the door of my bedroom after work, I'd fall to my knees to cry and pray. Whew, it was like a burden had been lifted from my shoulders. Wow! What a relief I thought. I'd felt life was being breathed back into me and joy was beginning to surround me more and more.

We'd begun to attend church a lot. So that we didn't have time to think about anything else. It seemed to be a revival every month and we didn't miss a beat. Every church service was like water upon a desert land. I couldn't wait to hear the sounds of praise that would erupt from the singers and musicians. I'd stand on every song as the melodies soothed my heart and mind. It wasn't long until we'd found our way to join the youth and young adult group. Everyone was so nice. Of course my husband knew almost everyone as he'd grown up there. His father was an Elder and his Grandfather was the Senior Pastor. My husband began to attend morning intercessory prayer and his passion for God was growing and growing. He'd already had a passion for the Word of God. I would see him reading and reading for hours. At times, I was a little jealous and tried to get his attention, but he was totally engulfed. So, I found myself being occupied more with studying the Word as well. I didn't realize it then, but as I reflect back, I can see that we both had found another passion and another love to fill what wasn't happening between us. It seemed like a happy place. I was able to cope and keep it moving.

I'd finally begun to lose those baby pounds, as I began to

incorporate a daily workout regimen and eating balanced proportioned meals. And then came the unexpected. The eyes of other men began to gaze. I acted as if it wasn't a big deal. I was happily married, saved, and a mom. I didn't dress provocative, so there is no reason they would really be drawn to me. Wrong. With each passing day, I'd receive a visitor at my job. It started with a friendly hello, then small talk. I honestly didn't really give it much thought, just figured people were just being nice. But after a while, something began to happen in my heart. I'd begun to have dreams that I wouldn't dare share with anyone, especially not my husband. It was if I couldn't shake the dreams. I'd question myself: Why were these dreams happening and why was I seeing the faces of the men I'd see along my day? I felt a little trapped within my own emotions, dreams, and imagination. There seemed to be no way out of this weird but somewhat flattering daydream. I found my heart pulling away more and more from my connection with my husband. We'd talk but not nearly as much about things that we used to talk about. You know, what's your favorite anything? Our flame was officially down to a mere ember. My heart sank as I thought about it.

Eye Shadow

We'd both found ourselves falling back into what was bringing us the most joy, and that was reading and studying the Word of God for hours and attending church services. As we totally dove into our connection with our church group, we began to be a great influence to many who would come. Our passion had begun to spill over onto the group, and the youth and young adults were experiencing a revival. We started leaving our Friday night fellowships at the church to start all over again at another member's home. We'd gather together to fellowship over food and great conversation. Soon after, my husband along with a few others, suggested that we come together to pray. And to my surprise, everyone agreed. We'd pray until the early hours of the morning, sometimes awaking to a full sunrise. We'd continue this fellowship week after week. Before we knew it, our fellowship had grown so much that the entire upstairs living, dining room, and basement was filled with youth. Soon, our youth group was set ablaze, and we all showed up to occupy the first three rows of the church. What an amazing time that was! Between us, our love and passion for each other had paled in comparison to our new found purpose in Christ. All of our energy, emotions, and passion was now poured into this new mission. I knew then that somehow the Lord was revealing to us our purpose in His kingdom. We were joined together for a purpose.

The distractions I had been experiencing at work, with the random visits by men, were now being blocked by this greater passion for seeking God that had been spun on by our fellowship with the youth and young adult group. It was like purpose had birth a new passion. A few months after, we'd found out that I was pregnant with our second child. What a joyous time, until time to go back to work. Now we were in over our heads for sure with two children and bills beyond belief. The struggle was real and we were holding on with everything to keep it together. We resorted to keeping our head into the Word of God and attending church often. I felt like we lived there. I had no complaints because it kept my mind occupied.

Then out of nowhere, my husband felt a call to go higher. He shared with me that he was going to resign his position as the church drummer and totally give himself to intercessory prayer. I thought ok, great. Three months later, he'd expressed that he felt a call to leave our home church. My heart sunk and the feeling of uncertainty came over me. I'd just gotten my everything stabilized and now this. Where would we go? What would occupy our time and energy? When Sunday rolled around, my husband decided he was not going to church that morning. I was determined that I was going to make my way to church without him that morning. Crazy thing happened; I'd gotten lost and ended up two exits away from where I really needed to be. Soon, I found myself driving on this long secluded road that seemed to lead to nowhere. Was this the Lord telling me something. I began to cry and go into a frenzy. Eventually, I found my way back to the beltway and going in the right direction toward home. As soon as I hit the front door, I told my husband that I tried to make it to church but got lost. I told him that I didn't understand how I got lost because we'd practically lived there. He chuckled, shook his head, and walked away. Then I thought, maybe this is a sign that our time there was up. That it was really time to find another place of worship.

That next week, I'd heard a pastor on the radio sharing about returning to prayer. His teachings drew me in and stirred my hunger for the Word of God. So I shared with my husband my experience in listening to this radio pastor and insisted that he tune in to hear him. And so he did just that. He expressed that he was really blessed by the message on the radio. So we both decided that we would go visit the church. After visiting the church, we soon became members. We partnered together in intercessory prayer and soon the church began to grow. Our fellowship moved from one very small conference room to a much larger conference room. People from everywhere began to attend. My heart felt purpose again and there was somewhat of a happy moment for me. We'd found a place where our passion for God could continue. So we attended regularly. It was a little different than what we were used to, but we found where we fit and stuck with it. We'd soon become licensed ministers and proudly assisted our pastor in whatever was needed to help the church grow.

We'd begun to make friends at our new church and found a way to occupy our time by connecting with them over dinner often. Still there was no time for each other, but we counted our lives to be surrendered totally to the Lord. There were times that my heart would long for love and passion in our marriage. My mind would, at times, take a pause and I'd think about what life would be like if I'd made another decision not to marry so young. I'd realized that the foundation of our decision to get married had changed and I no longer had the same passion for him as one in love. But quickly, I'd pushed those thoughts and feelings down and keep going. It seemed some days to be numb, like I was just going along to get along. In desperation, I would look for ways to connect with the one I'd once fallen in love with. So I'd spark up a conversation about the Word of God and we'd easily go on and on. It was obvious that we'd grown in our connection in faith, while our love connection was being greatly neglected. I couldn't figure it out; how could our connection in faith grow while our love connection diminishes? Were we lacking balance through it all?

One day as I looked in the mirror, I saw a changed woman; someone who didn't look like herself. Who was this woman? I looked like an old lady stuck in a holiness movement. I inhaled and exhaled as I felt this lost feeling coming over me. Was I really happy? Was I doing all of this to prove to others that I'm not a failure? What was happening to me? Who could I really talk to about what I was feeling?

With the turn of another season, I found myself pushing those feelings down and pushing along. My mom would call a lot to check on me. I felt like she knew what was going on with me, but didn't want to rattle the cage too much. So she would ask me to come over, just to get out of the house. I found myself escaping to her house just to do nothing but sit in front of the television for hours. I'd bring my children along because I didn't want my son to be bored, and surely I was not going to leave my new baby girl at home. And I really thought it was the right thing to do.

The funny thing, my husband continued his pursuit after God wholeheartedly. It was as if he'd blocked everything and everyone out. I remember telling him some days, "You think you're like Paul on the Isle of Patmos, don't you?" He'd smile and say, "Honey, what are you talking about?" I really meant it. It was like he was all alone, kind of in his own world. I sure felt like I was all alone. So, my once in a while trip to mom's turned into an every weekend adventure, just me and my children.

One evening my husband came home to tell me he'd lost all of his contracts, his work van was stolen, and he was unemployed. After a few weeks, I sat in my car and thought; I'm going to tell him to do what he is called to do. And so I did. His response was almost immediate. As his eyes got big, he agreed and told me that he felt led to start a Bible study. Ok, I responded. I didn't know what I'd just initiated and agreed to.

We'd talked about how we would present it to our pastor at the time. He was almost sure that our pastor would be so excited. So he scheduled to meet with him that next week. In preparing for our meeting, my husband believed that he was actually called to start a church. And so that was our agenda, to talk to our pastor about starting a church in our apartment. As we met with our pastor at his home to break the news, he began to give us this look of disappointment. He continued to listen as my husband adamantly tried to reason with him that this decision was from God. My husband even went as far as asking if he would be our covering. And BOOM, a thundering NO came forth; as our pastor disagreed with everything we were sharing. We didn't have his blessings that day, but within my heart I felt relieved that we wouldn't have to drive 45 minutes to church anymore. I was a little disappointed that he wouldn't even take the opportunity to mentor us and push us along. Oh well, on to the next.

So my husband, I, and our family started our next chapter in purpose, starting our first church together. I'll never forget the very first Sunday. It was me, my two little children, and four other friends sitting on our couch; all dressed up listening to my husband teach and preach the Word in our one bedroom apartment. What a humble beginning, I would say. Some of our friends from the church we just left began to inquire about this new work. Some even came to visit for a few Sundays. Oh, what an encouragement for the both of us! We were so excited! It wasn't long until a very close friend came and actually joined our fellowship. He was such an encouragement to my husband. He and my husband built a very special bond almost like Jonathan and David in the Bible. He needed this connection, to keep him going forward. Before long, people began to join the fellowship coming from all over the area.

Then the unexpected began to happen. As people began to join, I felt alone again. My husband now had a new best friend for which he shared his passion for God with; and I just stayed in my own little bubble with just me and my two children. I found myself revisiting the place where I was seeking to gain the attention of my husband, but it seemed to me that all he was really in to was the church he was now pastoring. All of his energy, time, and passion was now being poured into the church and the needs of the new members. I was happy and sad at the same time I guess; happy because his dreams were coming to pass, but sad that there was still no passion between us. I began to despise having church in my home and sometimes wished that we'd just live a normal life again. He was only receiving a small love gift for preaching and I was the only one able to pay the bills. I never forget telling him, "You'd saved the world with no money if you could," and practically, he was doing just that. It was at that point where I was being questioned by my closest relatives about my husband's lack of income. I was constantly grilled about our means of income. It was at that point where I couldn't take it any longer. I became mean and resented the fact that I had to work hard just to pay the bills and put food in our children's mouths. I resented the fact that I was giving and giving and receiving nothing in return. I would have these heart to heart talks with my husband while crying uncontrollably. He seemed not to be moved by my anguish, my hurt, my depression, and my resentment. He'd always ended our conversation with, "The Lord will provide." Urrrr…I hated that statement with a passion.

I started up the visits to mom's house again. She could tell right away that I was angry about something. She would ask me am I ok. I couldn't reveal to her how I really felt because that would have meant that she was right and I was wrong about marrying too young. So I bottled it up, having no one and nowhere to release this burden. I began to stuff my feelings down and looked for ways to keep my sanity, so I continued seeking the Lord and even started a women's fellowship. But that soon became a burden as I couldn't take the feeling of rejection from those who felt a need to challenge me on every hand. It just wasn't helping and filling the emptiness I continued to feel inside. I started working late hours and accepting projects on purpose, just to avoid home, specifically on the nights we were having church services. It seemed like I was grasping to find a way to cope again with what I was going through.

One night, I couldn't take it any longer; I confronted my husband one last time about him getting a job to help with the bills. He so calmly stated, "The Lord will provide." That was it, I'd had enough. I stood up and said, "I was here before any of these people were here and let's see if they will provide." I packed my bags and grabbed our children and headed for my mom's house. I was done. As I drove over the first speed bump, I felt like I was being freed from a cage. As I kept driving, I didn't even think to look back. I just wanted my life to be normal again. I just wanted to be happy again.

Two months had passed and my husband would come by to visit every day. It was like old times. He'd used to come by almost every evening when we were just dating, just to talk about anything. And now it was like de ja vu, or more like we'd been given another try at falling in love again. My heart began to melt and a fire was being rekindled again within our hearts. I was really liking this new love reconnection. The way he looked at me with those dreamy eyes, I couldn't resist blushing as he would tell me how much he missed me. Funny thing is, my mom would be watching from the window, or from the side of the house, or from the garage. She'd warned him not to even come up in the driveway. Bless her heart. She would always fight tooth and nail for us. I love my mom so much. I laugh today, thinking about how she is such an awesome protector. And she will still protect now, if anyone crosses her babies, well the grandbabies have stolen her heart now, and they are her new mission.

By the third month at my mom's house, I was so miserable. I couldn't fight it. It was as if something inside was saying you were made for each other. I just knew either I was losing it, or just maybe it was an answered prayer. After that, I'd made up my mind that I was going back home. So I did. I called up my husband to tell him the good news and he made his way over there in a flash. We packed everything in the car and headed back home. In those three months while we were apart, God did something in our hearts and helped us to mend our marriage. We'd found our love again. We went back to the foundations of our love and began to rebuild again.

Lipstick

On my journey, I found that young love is beautiful, but can also be quite challenging. Life has a way of throwing a couple of curveballs that we often are not ready for, especially in marriage. There is so much that I had to learn about keeping the flame of love going in our marriage, and it wasn't in my going to every church service, serving people, or even trying to measure up to the one I'd fallen in love with. It took us returning to the place where we first fell in love; where all outside events, circumstances, and activities took the back seat to our efforts of rekindling our love for one another. There is a wonderful scripture that is filled with wisdom that I stand on during shaky times.

Catch the foxes for us, the little foxes that spoil the vineyards, for our vineyards are in blossom. Songs of Solomon 2:15 ESV

This verse reminds me that we must be diligent together about keeping the little foxes out of our garden of Love. The little foxes of busyness, selfishness, lack of communication, lack of concern for one another, lack of intimacy, other people's ungodly opinions, and a lack of wise counsel can cause what we once had to become an empty field for weeds to grow.

Would I change my decision to get married young, probably not, but if I had the opportunity to change how I handled my grief and heart ache, I would have done so. I found later on in life that it's ok to admit that you don't have it all together, even as a Christian, and that it's more than ok to find that person that you can connect with and confide in about your struggles for the purpose of helping you through life's challenges. I found that the Word of God gives insight on this matter in Titus 2:4-5.

That they may teach the young women to be sober, to love their husbands, to love their children, To be discreet, chaste, keepers at home, good, obedient to their own husbands, that the word of God be not blasphemed. Titus 2:4-5 KJV

This verse is referring to the older women teaching the younger women how to be balanced in every area of their life with God as their foundation. Being married and being a mother at such a young age meant that I had to miss out on some things; it meant that I ultimately had to grow up and become responsible for me and someone else. I didn't understand that I would have to intentionally be organized and at times miss even a few church revivals to ensure that my home, my husband, my children, and even myself was properly cared for.

There is a special verse that I stumble upon during my last pregnancy that continually rings in my heart and helps me to stay before the Lord and to keep my ears open to instructions whispered by wise women. It is Proverbs 14:1:

Every wise woman buildeth her house: but the foolish pluketh it down with her hands. Proverbs 14:1 KJV

I realized that God has given me the ability and the wherewithal, to turn a house into a home, and He's allowed me to see who I am and the strength I have through the many wise women who I eventually allowed to encourage me, pray for me, and guide me along the way. By just allowing my walls to come down and my heart to be open to the wise counsel of seasoned women of God, I became that wise woman, who knows now not to walk away or give up when times are hard, but to seek the Lord, confront with wisdom, and do what I can do to build my house. I had to also take a moment to look within, and I found that I was a little self-centered and a little codependent. These two are not a good pair for a wife and a mother to have. I'd learned through days of disappointment that I had to become more independent with regards to taking care of my natural house as well as my spiritual house. Waiting around for someone to do something didn't always work in my favor or in the favor of the functioning of our home. I had to identify the places where I could complement our partnership in marriage and building a happy home. What I longed for, I could list it down, pray about it, talk to the seasoned women of God, and allow the creative side of me to come forward. I also learned that things could be done in stages and phases. Everything doesn't change overnight but with a plan, it can happen; your plan can become a reality.

I would often think of the Proverbs 31 women and how she seemed to have it all together and I'd instantly lose the battle; but in reading and fellowshipping with a few seasoned women, I realized that with each season and with time, this Proverbs 31 woman had managed to create her regimen whereby her home could properly function. She even took a moment to realize her worth enough to treat herself at times by clothing herself with beautiful attire. Most of all what I admired most about this Proverbs 31 woman was that she allowed God to work on her inner self to shape and fashion her to be an awesome reflection of who He is in the earth.

Charm is deceitful and beauty is vain, but a woman who fears the Lord is to be praised. Proverbs 31:30 ESV

Oh when I reflect back, I see that God's divine hand was on our marriage and on every obstacle we faced. Did He see us in our toughest times? I believe He did. But I also believe that the Lord knew just how much we could bare and was preparing a Run Away Bride to become a Virtuous Woman.

Today, we are intentional about keeping our flame of love burning by spending quality time together with each other. We welcome balance as it helps us to continue to walk together in our purpose to glorify God and to stay passionately in love with one another.

We are now 19 years married with now three beautiful children, and we are also 14 years serving as pastors together. Our oldest son is 19-years-old, in school and working a lucrative job. He also is walking beside us in ministry at our church. My daughter is 17 and a senior in high school. She is an honor student and looking forward to attending college. She is planning to become the next highest paid CPA in the Washington Metropolitan area. And my youngest son is 9- years-old and is keeping us busy all day, every day. What a joy!

I am proud to say that running away is no longer my answer. It wasn't always this way but somehow, by the grace of God, I have gained strength within that I know only God almighty has given me over the years. The reality is, a wise woman truly does have what it takes to make a house a home, by God's amazing grace. It's not necessarily what someone else can do to make it work; it's what you can do, by the grace of God, that will make it work.

PASTOR ADRIAN PARTLOW
Community Temple Bible Way Church
6207 State Street
Cheverly MD 20785
www.adrianpartlowministries.org
womensheartministry@hotmail.com
301-367-9930

Elder Partlow acknowledged God's call on her life in 1999 and preached her initial sermon on December 13, 1999. She was licensed as an Evangelist in July 2000 at the Bible Way Worldwide Holy Convocation. She was ordained Elder in July 2003 and in July 2010 she was installed as Assistant Pastor, under the tutelage of Bishop Robert A. Pitts of Community Temple Bible Way Church of Cheverly, Maryland.

Elder Partlow has been a member of the Community Temple Bible Way Church for 33 years under the leadership of Bishop Robert A. Pitts and First Lady Esther Pitts, where she serves as the Assistant Pastor, Church Administrator, Chair of the Ministerial Board, Financial Board member, Tuesday's Night Word Empowerment Facilitator and Director/ Instructor of the Divine Order School of Ministry which she started in February 2007. Elder Partlow is also the Founder and Director of the Women's Heart Ministry, a mentoring ministry for women. Many have been developed into ministry through training and encouraged through the women's ministry.

In 1999, Elder Partlow began her biblical studies and ministerial training at Jericho Bible College, Shiloh School of Ministry, Calvary Bible Institute, Logos Christian College, Washington Saturday College (Howard University). She is currently pursuing a Bachelor of Arts Degree/Certification in Christian Counseling and Pastoral Care at Cornerstone University. She is employed with the U.S. Department of State as a Management Analyst for 22 years. She has carried the Word of God into conferences, women's retreats, nursing homes, street ministry, bible studies on her job, in her home and had the opportunity to minister in Ghana, Africa in April 2014 where souls were saved, set free and delivered.

Elder Partlow has a deep burden for souls, and desires to see the body of Christ empowered to live victoriously and abundantly, free from the power of the enemy. She lives by her scriptural motto, found in I Corinthians 9:19, "For though I be free from all men, yet have I made myself servant unto all, that I might gain the more."

I NEVER GAVE YOU PERMISSION

Psalm 94:17
Unless the Lord had given me help, I would soon have dwelt in the silence of death.

Psalm 120:1
In my distress I cried to the Lord, and heard me.

I was raised as the only child. I have been in church all of my life which includes that I am a preacher's kid... My parents were foster parents for over 20 years and by the time I graduated from high school they adopted five children. I grew up with many challenges of being told that I was too young to serve God and that I needed to have my fun. I was called a holy roller. I struggled with not being able to hang out with my friends like I wanted to as they were being very promiscuous and doing things that would label them for the rest of their lives. My parents were very protective of me. I wasn't privy to a lot of overnight stays at my girlfriend's house and going to the different concerts and go-go bands. Yes, I thought my parents were very strict and couldn't understand why I couldn't do certain things that I thought was the normal things to do as a child.

I was a child that didn't need a lot of attention. I didn't bother anybody; I always was minding my business. I found out I was picked out to be picked on. It didn't seem to be enough for my neighborhood friends. They would always find a way to instigate a situation to cause people to say things about me and then come run to me to say they were talking about you and then it was you need to fight them. I found myself fighting people that I really liked because my so-called friends thought it was a good thing to fight this person off of the bus. Later, I was the one in trouble with my parents because I wasn't given permission to fight.

Every summer during my elementary school age and school was out, it was my parent's routine to take me to one of my grandparent's home every day during the week until they got off of work. It was a time that I enjoyed, since I love to spend time with my grandmothers. From cooking me breakfast with the grits, eggs, bacon, and a cup of coffee, those are the times I cherish.

During those summer visits, there were family members who were there and they always felt thrilled to be able to play with me and make my life what they called exciting. From scaring me to death to exploring some things that I now realize was not appropriate, I never thought this experience would make me to be able to identify who I was; to think that these experiences would be caused by those who I loved to take advantage of who I am and what I was becoming.

As I look back over my life, I see how the devil was trying to create what he wanted me to be versus what God has called me to be. Those special trips to the overnight sleepovers where a family member couldn't wait for the lights to go out at night to get me out of bed, to do what he thought was the right thing to do to make him feel good; not caring how inappropriate his behavior was.

Being young, I thought this is the way love was supposed to be shown. How did you think that I was your girlfriend when I was indeed your family? I really thought this was okay to do, but I never understood why I was the one to be picked out to be picked on. This violation of my body caused me to be embarrassed to undress in front of my mother and my girlfriends to cause me to have a complex about myself. It was my only way to let people know that it was my body if only I had control of it.

I never gave anyone permission to touch me in a way that made me feel uncomfortable. I never gave anyone permission to make me dress with the lights off. I never gave anyone permission the right to make me feel that I was a rag that could be used at any given time that made me feel good.

Why couldn't I just be accepted the way I was? I was told that I would never amount to anything. Is that why the devil was so strong in trying to attack my family?

It wasn't until I got older to be an adult that I realized that those things that happened in my life were not supposed to happen and that it was indeed wrong. There was a statement by one of my accusers that told my husband that he was surprised that I didn't have a house full of children. It hurt me to my heart because the things he did do to me, did not determine what my future would be according to his eyes. What the devil meant for evil, God turned it around for my good!
At the age of 11- years-old, the Lord came into my life and filled me with the precious Holy Ghost. I am thankful because I see how life was trying to turn me into different a direction that would not have been pleasing to God.

God had a purpose for my life that I was not aware of at that time. I knew I was different from all of the others. Under the tutelage of my parents, I developed a prayer life that I never knew would help me through a lot of turmoil and obstacles that I thought I would never face, but God has brought me through victoriously.

As a little girl, there was a song that I would sing for the late Bishop Arthur Pressley named, "Jesus Loves Me," that song brought me through a lot of sad times for me when I would feel a certain a way. I don't t care what I would go through, but as long as I knew Jesus loved me, nothing else matter.

BROKEN VESSELS, SHATTERED VOWS!

Psalm 31

In you, Lord, have I taken refuge; let me never be put to shame; deliver me in your righteousness. Incline your ear to me; make haste to deliver me. Be my strong rock, a fortress to save me, for you are my rock and my stronghold; guide me, and lead me for your name's sake. Take me out of the net that they have laid secretly for me, for you are my strength. Into your hands I commend my spirit, for you have redeemed me, O Lord God of truth. I hate those who cling to worthless idols; I put my trust in the Lord. I will be glad and rejoice in your mercy, for you have seen my affliction and known my soul in adversity. You have not shut me up in the hand of the enemy; you have set my feet in an open place. Have mercy on me, Lord, for I am in trouble; my eye is consumed with sorrow, my soul and my body also. For my life is wasted with grief, and my years with sighing; my strength fails me because of my affliction, and my bones are consumed. I have become a reproach to all my enemies and even to my neighbors, an object of dread to my acquaintances; when they see me in the street they flee from me. I am forgotten like one that is dead, out of mind; I have become like a broken vessel. For I have heard the whispering of the crowd; fear is on every side; they scheme together against me, and plot to take my life. But my trust is in you, O Lord. I have said, 'You are my God. 'My times are in your hand; deliver me from the hand of my enemies, and from those who persecute me. Make your face to shine upon your servant, and save me for your mercy's sake. Lord, let me not be confounded for I have called upon you; but let the wicked be put to shame; let them be silent in the grave. Let the lying lips be put to silence that speak against the righteous with arrogance, disdain and contempt. How abundant is your goodness, O Lord, which you have laid up for those who fear you; which you have prepared in the sight of all for those who put their trust in you. You hide them in the shelter of your presence from those who slander them; you keep them safe in your refuge from the strife of tongues. Blessed be the Lord! For he has shown me his steadfast love when I was as a city besieged. I had said in my alarm, I have been cut off from the sight of your eyes. Nevertheless, you heard the voice of my prayer when I cried out to you. Love the Lord, all you his servants; for the Lord protects the faithful, but repays to the full the proud. Be strong and let your heart take courage, all you who wait in hope for the Lord.

After a lengthy relationship and being promiscuous, I got pregnant at 18- years- old. The original decision was to abort the pregnancy. I was prepared and ready to get things taken care of. It was that morning of the procedure, the Lord placed in my spirit not to go through with it and that my child would be a blessing to me. I held on to what I heard in my spirit and didn't go through with the abortion. Boy, did that take a shift in people's hearts. It was one of the best decisions that I could have made in my life. Later on in the relationship, the decision was made to make things right by getting married. It was a relationship that I thought was a match made from heaven, but at times life throws us a curveball.

I was living the life that I thought I knew how to live without any instructions in how to do and what not to do. Sometimes folks just think you know by the examples that they think were given. Being pregnant and married was not easy, neither was it comfortable for me. It seem like a marriage without total dependence on God, but what we felt, we wanted to do on our own terms regardless of what the repercussion would be.

My firstborn was welcomed into this world on January 14, 1987. I didn't know that my marriage was being tested in a way that would cause me to be broken in a way that drained me emotionally, mentally, physically, and spiritually. Being very young in marriage, I didn't have people that I could talk to because all of my friends were not married. When I would share, those so-called friends would talk about me behind my back and make jokes about my relationship which caused me to be even more broken.

After one year of marriage, infidelity entered into my marriage that was causing my vows to be shattered. I couldn't understand this process of marriage since this was my first intimate relationship to the man I love. How could this happen? What is wrong with me? What did I do or go wrong? From that point of my life, everything was going downhill.

I finally woke up out of my stupor when I was told, "I got what I wanted out of you and I have now messed your life up!!!" This is when I got a new lease on my life. The devil thought he had me, but I got away. I came to grips to say, Lord, I deserve better in life. Lord, I am all yours and

I know you are with me. Two years later, I was divorced and I went through a time thinking that I had missed out on life. I told the Lord that I felt like I never experienced anything to be able to tell anybody anything about life. I said, "Lord, make my life an example." I really didn't know what I was asking, but I went through some things in life that caused me even more brokenness. I was looking for wholeness in relationships that could not give me the fulfillment that I needed. I was in a relationship that was against what I believe. My thoughts were not to change him and him not to change me. I didn't have a clue what was taking place around me. I just know now that I could have been killed, but God covered me because that guy is now dead in his grave and God has allowed me to live. I began to go clubbing and drinking to fit in a crowd that was different from my upbringing, until one day I got so drunk that I thought my life was about to end. I told God if you would bring me out of this, I promise I would not go back to that lifestyle. I realized that the devil was trying to steal, kill, and destroy me and I was giving him the power to do so. It was one Sunday morning, I went to church and I sat there and as the word was going forth, the word was pricking my heart and the Lord spoke to me, "Whom are you going to serve? Me or the devil?" My life changed that day and I told the Lord I will serve you for the rest of my life.

I was able to come out of this as pure gold. I am grateful for my family who was right there for me to help me raise my son. The Lord has always provided me with good jobs to provide for my son without any public assistance. It pays to serve God. If you take care of God's business, He will take care of yours. I wasn't the perfect mother, but I am grateful for my oldest son and how God has kept him through my shortcomings. Being young, I made a lot of mistakes and bad choices that I had to pay for, but God has kept me through this process. The devil tried to kill two birds with one stone, but God blocked it.

NEW PHASE

Revelation 22:1 Then he showed me a river of the water of life, clear as crystal, coming from the throne of God and of the Lamb.

I am now walking into this new phase of my life, but I am still bitter in some aspects of my life because I had not forgiven the people in my prior life of relationships. I was hurt, abused, and betrayed. I felt like I had missed so much of my young life. I had to go back to my previous relationships and ask for forgiveness. Also, I am able to face my accusers that I never gave permission to hurt and abuse me and say I am free.

When all else failed, God stood by me. After all I had been through, not even given it a thought to start another relationship, God had another plan for my life. On September 29, 1990, I married my middle school classmate, Clyde Partlow, Jr. My union was extended with my daughter, Jasmine Partlow and another son Clyde Partlow III. This new phase has not been an easy task and brought about new challenges, but God has brought me through the trials and tribulations. I understand why I had to go through what I have been through because God called me into ministry in 1999. It was only the beginning. This process has tested my marriage and relationship with my children to the point of almost to losing every last one of them. God is a restorer! I have learned to not take all things personal, but it is to make you what God wants you to be.

We think sometimes that things won't repeat or recycle, but it does. You can't leave things empty, but we have to deal with it at some point in our lives. My marriage was tested when my husband walked out of my life for a season. I had no knowledge of where he was. I was confused and broken again because I didn't once again understand this process of my life. It was a testing of my faith to see where my relationship was with God. There are times when we take God for granted as well as people. I preach so many times, that at some points in our lives that we might have to walk alone. Well, I never thought I was preaching to myself. When I say, I've walked alone, it was just me. I told myself, what are you going to do now? When I would come home to an empty house, I would say, "Where Are You God? Can I do this all by myself? How can I make it?" God showed Himself faithful in a way that He took care of me mentally, physically, spiritually, and financially. He promised that He would be with me always even to the end of the world.

This is where the Lord was really pruning me a way where I was truly hurt to the core. It seemed like everything that was close to me was against me and was trying me in every aspects of my life. I had to question God to see if He really called me into ministry. He showed me that I wasn't my own, but I was His. I had to get to that point to believe that God truly meant what He had promised me. I began to walk my faith and not my sight. This road was hard and very blurry. I couldn't see the end. Many days and nights I wanted to give up on my marriage, but God wouldn't give me the release that I expected. Once again, I had to set myself in position in the posture of prayer. I started walking in the attitude of prayer. I started speaking those things not as they were but as they are. I had to pick my position and not listen to the noise. The devil told me that I wouldn't survive the second time around, but I stood up and told myself, I am more than a conqueror through Jesus Christ who loves me. What the devil meant for evil, God turned it around for my good!

This new phase has opened up many doors for me that I didn't see before. It has allowed my ministry to broaden in ways that I know it is all good and all God.

There were expectations from people who thought, I will fail and I would never be anything. How can this young girl survive this trial and tribulation? Will she have a comeback? Being faithful and obedience to God and ministry has really gotten me through a lot. Isaiah 1:19-20 says that if ye be willing and obedient, ye shall eat the good of the land. But if ye refuse and rebel, ye shall be devoured with the sword: for the mouth of the LORD hath spoken it.

I realize I am not perfect and I still have a long way to go, but God is bringing me through this season of my life, with a new mindset and a higher level of faith. Without faith it is impossible to please God! My story has encouraged others that God can bring you out of any situation victorious! You don't have to die, but you will live! God has been my provider, my healer, and my deliverer. What a Mighty God I Serve!

I see the things of God unfolding before me. There are times that I stand in awe of God because I feel I am deserving of it and it can't before. When you have been used and abused for such a long time, you began to believe that nothing good can come your way. I always can believe for someone else, but always see less for myself. For so long I hid, "Behind My Make-Up" and not giving the real me because I thought the make-up is what folks really wanted to see. I just wanted to stay in my make-up case. It made me feel confined. God was showing me who I was and the power He has invested in me and my life, but being woman it just couldn't be so. Exodus 3:14 says And God said unto Moses, I AM THAT I AM: and he said, Thus shall thou say unto the children of Israel, I AM hath sent me unto you.

When God speaks, it is my cue to move to where God wants me and just tell me, "Yes." He doesn't have to tell me twice. He is a God of a second chance. I am so glad that He looked beyond my faults and saw my needs. I ask the Lord to make me out of example so that I would have a testimony to tell the world. It is my assignment to tell the story everywhere I go so that those can be healed, set free, and delivered. The harvest is ripe, but the laborers are few. I want to be one of the few to bring those who are hungry to the knowledge of Christ.

I give thanks to all of my children, Jasmine, Clyde III, and Malcolm Jr. They have seen the real me, "Behind My Make-up." There are many times they didn't understand why I allowed myself to go through what I been through and not understanding it was my process that God was taking me through. All they could see that I was strong and I kept on standing. It was my prayer that my children would see that I never gave up on God even when there were days and nights that my daughter would see me crying and praying. I just believe that God's will is going to be done. If He said it, I believe it, and that settles it!

Don't allow your circumstances to dictate your future. God is in control!
Proverbs 3:5-6 says Trust in the Lord with all your heart and do not lean on your own understanding. In all your ways acknowledge Him, and He will make your paths straight. It is not about you, but all about Christ! When we take ourselves out of the equation, we can see God more in what He is trying to do to make us what He want us to be.

Tell your story! Somebody's life is depending upon it. When you don't tell it, there are people who are dying. How much will your make-up cover you because it is never permanent? In the heat of the moment, make-up will begin to wash away and then people will see the real you, especially when you are not looking. God has given us all an assignment, but you must accomplish the test before you so that your assignment can be completed. The race is not given, to the swift nor to the strong but the one who endureth to the end. There is a NEW PHASE that you must enter, what are YOU waiting for? Get from Behind The Makeup!

Pastor Vondale Mack
Kingdom of Priest Ministry Center
P.O. Box 47523
District Heights, MD 20747
Pastorvondale@gmail.com
(301)322-2790

The CEO and Founder of In His Presence Outreach Center, Vondale is a woman of God, who is a servant at heart. Her first ministry is to her husband Pastor Gregory Mack, Sr. and their three children Gregory Jr., Jonaya, and Marcellous Mack. Vondale is a native of Prince George's County Maryland. Her education has earned her the following accolades: a Child Development Certificate to work with children with Motor Skills Disabilities; and Associates of Arts & Science degree in Criminal Justice for Prince Georges' Community College; induction into Alpha Chi Honor Society; and a Bachelor of Science in Sociology degree with a Minor in Criminal Justice (Cum Laude) from Bowie State University.

In July 2012 after faithfully serving at Kingdom of Priests Community Church (KOP), she was ordained Pastor. In 2014, KOP launched community cell groups to help bridge the gap between community and kingdom. During these gatherings many families have been restored, souls saved, and mind sets changed. KOP has partnered with Martha's Table, CAFY, Salvation Army, Sistas United, Inc., and Cancer Support Foundation to provide food, clothing, and toys for families less fortune. Vondale has volunteered in various capacities in Prince George's County, including ten years as an advocate for victims of abuse. She was also a Victim Service Manager for Community Advocates for Family and Youth (CAFY) where she worked with the Homicide and Armed Robbery Division, and served as supervisor for 24hr Help Line to help victims of Domestic Violence. She served on the Domestic Violence Coordinating Council, and has facilitated and spoken at numerous conferences and workshops to help educate and empower women and youth on abuse and bullying. In 2007, she was awarded the Volunteer Presidential Award from former President George W. Bush. In October 2012, she received her National Advocate Credentials as a "Comprehensive Victim Intervention Specialist" from the National Organization for Victim Assistance. In 2015, she was awarded the Presidential Group A ward from President Barack Obama for her dedication to helping organize Walk A Mile In My Shoes Annual Walk to help bring comfort, support, and encouragement to those who lost loved ones to violence. Vondale makes each victim her number one priority, as a survivor of sexual assault she knows the impact crime has on your life. She often says she is so loud because at once she was forced to be silent. She now speaks not just for herself but those forced to suffer in silence.

Vondale currently serves on several boards Kingdom of Priest Ministry Center, In His Presence Outreach Center, 3Fish 5loaves, and Sistas United, Inc.

She declares, "To everything there is a time and season for everything, but when it links up you need to seize the moment!"

BEHIND THE MAKEUP

THE ALLURE OF UNCLEAN HONEY

Judges 14:9 (NIV) *"He scooped out the honey with his hands and ate as he went along. When he rejoined his parents, he gave them some, and they too ate it. But he did not tell them that he had taken the honey from the lion's carcass."*

Many of us read this scripture in disgust. How could Samson not only partake of something so contaminated and vile, but also share it with his loved ones? The truth of the matter is that some of us have done just that. We have disobeyed the Holy Spirit by lying, stealing, and deceiving to enjoy a sweet yet unsavory and unholy taste. Delilah wasn't the only woman to use her "honey pot" to seduce a man in order to retrieve information, distract, or steal. People think that if you are a pastor or first lady, then you are exempt from hardship, distractions, and temptations. In fact, you are more prone to it. I don't care what position or title you hold, if you are not steadfast in prayer and fully submitted to the unction of the Holy Ghost, you can find yourself in a real dilemma. I am a witness…

Lipstick

Honey (noun) – An excellent example of something.

It was the summer of 1993 when my husband and I first laid eyes on each other. We were at Landover Mall, and I thought he had the brightest eyes and the most beautiful smile in the world. He was wearing a light blue, pink, and white striped Polo shirt, nice jeans, fresh 996 New Balance shoes, and a baseball cap. Although he was a rough neck, he had an innocence about him that captivated me. We didn't know it that first day, but our meeting was not by chance. It was in God's divine plan.

Both of us were just getting out of long-term relationships and really didn't expect much from the other, but the chemistry between us was strong and intense. We would talk for hours on the phone or sit outside on the rooftop. He cared about the things that concerned me and desired to meet my needs. I will never forget the time he drove in a blizzard to bring me a pizza with everything on it! It was a defining moment in our relationship. I learned a few things that day. 1) Be specific about what I tell him, because my idea of everything on a pizza didn't include black olives and anchovies. 2) This guy really loved me. 3) He would literally weather a storm to make me happy. It became apparent that in each other, we had found our soulmates. He was 20 and I was 17. Together, we believed that we could conquer the world.

I was in awe of this man! He had a natural swagger – subtle but sure. He had the look of a choirboy, but he was fearless like Bumpy Johnson (Fishburne, Laurence, Perf. *Hoodlum: Movie.* Dir. Bill Duke. United Artists, 1997, Film.) When he walked in a room, his presence commanded respect. I knew he was different from the type of hustlers I usually attracted, but I soon found out that I was wrong. He sold drugs and made fast money. *Unclean.*

However, he wanted a fresh start, and so did I. We were free enough and trusted each other enough to share our childhood trauma with one another. Our past adversities brought us closer together. I bared my soul to him, and I shared with him my painful experience of being molested by an older male cousin – my father's nephew.

He scooped out the honey with his hands…

The first time I was violated, I was just nine years old and at my grandmother's house. The abuse continued for a few years. Those experiences stripped me of my power, peace, and dignity and left me with fear, anger, disappointment, shame, and even lust. I grew into a cold and distant young woman. I wasn't going to allow anyone to make any more unwanted deposits in my life, so I took control of me. I built walls with those closest to me. I lashed out with my fists and my tongue. I had also become good friends with the spirit of manipulation. Throughout it all, I always prayed, but didn't have a personal relationship with God. I knew that despite what I was going through, He was with me. *"For I know the plans I have for you," declares the LORD, "plans to prosper you and not to harm you, plans to give you hope and a future.* (Jeremiah 29:11).

Maybe this is why I felt "My Guy" was sent from heaven, because our connection seemed supernatural. God knew all the pain I was going through and wouldn't allow someone else to take advantage of me. I felt myself letting down my guard and opening up my heart. My prince had arrived and in my new love's arms – I was safe and I was secure. He reassured me that I was the perfect girl for him, and he wasn't interested in anyone else. He wouldn't let anything happen to me. He protected me. He loved me. He covered me.

On July 12, 1997, we were joined in marriage. Although we had both become saved, neither of us still had a clue that God had us on His mind to help advance His Kingdom. In those early years, we had a loving relationship. We supported each other, complimented each other daily, and said, 'I love you' often in both word and deed. We rarely argued, and when we did – we settled any disagreements before we went to bed. Sleeping on the couch or walking on egg shells in our home was not an option. I trusted him 100%.

God's hand was upon our union, and we were living our dream in the early years. We had three children, were activate members in church, winning souls for Christ, having regular date nights, enjoying great sex, and working on establishing a legacy that would surpass us after we leave this earth. I was so ecstatic, because by this time we had made it beyond year five in our marriage. Many people said if we made it to the year of GRACE, then we could withstand anything. That theory would surely be tested several years later as our dream morphed into a nightmare…

Our relationship started to shift and not in the right direction. Things happened slowly. It was the small things at first. *"Catch for us the foxes, the little foxes that ruin the vineyards, our vineyards that are in bloom.* (Song of Solomon 2:15). For years, we prayed together every night, but at some point, we stopped. It wasn't that we ceased communicating with God individually, but we failed to realize how spending time in prayer as a couple was just as or more important as sex. Our intimacy suffered. We weren't affectionate. Our daily phone calls vanished, and our texting diminished. My husband started changing and going back to some of his old ways. He started staying out late, hanging with the "old crowd," and becoming distant.

Eventually, my husband backslid, which opened the door to inappropriate relationships with women, drinking, gambling, lying, deceiving, mishandling of finances, and the list goes on and on. I couldn't believe that I was sleeping with the enemy. I was doing everything I knew to do: pray, fast, submit, seek counseling, engage in sex, cook, clean, and give him space. I repeatedly tried to keep the lines of communication open. We had a lot of work to do in order to repair our marriage and I thought we both were willing to do whatever it took to make it happen, but that wasn't the case. I walked the "Hall of Shame," as I call it, every Sunday with my children. Everyone kept telling me, *"BE PATIENT"* and *"TRUST GOD."* "Blessed is the man who makes the Lord His trust…" I just wanted to scream! I know the Word, and I had been trusting in Him. That was the reason I was still married! I also know that trusting in God is a decision we all have to do daily. Dealing with marital issues, money problems, and mistrust is always challenging, but when you add children, ministry, and community outreach, it becomes overwhelming.

After a while, my husband returned to God and our relationship got better. However, many things stayed the same. Ephesians 4:26-27 states: *"In your anger do not sin; Do not let the sun go down while you are still angry, and do not give the devil a foothold."* Once we had lived by this scripture, but we had come to blatantly disobey it. We left the door wide open for the enemy and he strolled right in. The fresh aroma of grace that had permeated our home had been replaced by the stench of sin, and no matter how many candles burned, air fresheners hung, or fragrance sprayed, we couldn't remove the odor. While the spirits of peace, longsuffering, joy, and unity began to vacate, the spirits of disappointment, discouragement, resentment, anger, discord, and instant gratification had begun to move their luggage in and set up camp. These spirits not only started taking over our house, but our marriage. Both of us adopted a victim mentality, and each felt disrespected by the other.

My old companion, the spirit of manipulation, had not only returned but was operating fully in our home. Both my husband and I were pointing our fingers at each other, instead of taking truthful looks at ourselves. We began a vicious cycle of playing "the blame game" that continued for years. The walls that my husband had been able to tear down in me were being re-fortified and not in a good way. The safety that I felt was no longer there, so I retreated to a familiar and destructive place. I became cold, controlling, and callous, which caused him to become silent, withdrawn, lonely, and reckless, but we continued to present a united front in public.

We had mastered being great ministry partners: he, the outstanding teacher and I, the charismatic preacher. When I walked in the church, I could separate the disappointment of being his wife from the satisfaction of being his Kingdom co-laborer. I learned how to check my emotions and leave "house stuff" at the door. I took pride in seeing him walk in the authority of God, but simultaneously couldn't comprehend why he was not displaying those same qualities and determination in our home.

From the outside, we were picture perfect. People marveled at how this young couple with children was working for the Lord. Everyone said, "He's so powerful. He really knows how to break down the Word. That young guy is really going to do some great things for GOD." Meanwhile, I was seething at how he would pay careful attention to the needs of the ministry, but ignore the fact that his wife was dying on the inside. I was trying to be a good wife, but I didn't want to be picture perfect anymore. I knew that if anyone looked too closely, they'd see the cracks in the frame.

Our marriage had become a rollercoaster ride with countless ups and downs. I knew he was a good father and we co-parented well, but I needed more. Was it time to get off this ride? I added up the cost and had decided that it was time for me to get a "Frozen" anointing and "Let It Go!" After I graduated in May, I would start my new chapter and this meant closing the door on our marriage. My goal was for me to have all the separation papers signed by the fall.

January 5, 2006 "Dear Diary…The New Year is in full affect, and people are focused on making vows to start fresh. Old dreams are being revisited and new life is beginning for others. We are now into our fourth day of the consecration, and the temptation the last few months the enemy has sent to me has had me on my toes. The spirit of lust is trying to take me down. Although I'm running for my life, I must admit that I feel weak. I'm praying that the Father will renew my mind during this season. I have been trying to exercise and read the Book of Proverbs to take my mind off the eye candy that keeps running through my mind. He stands about 6'2, cinnamon brown skin, broad chest, shoulder length dreads, and those guns (biceps)! My heart doesn't want him but my body screams come get me. The devil truly has a trap set for me with all of his tricks. I see him watching me as a lion about to jump on his prey. Your heart does not want me, but your body needs me. I feel the heat of summer, but we are clearly in the midst of winter. LORD HELP ME!!! Every time I see him, I turn and walk the other way because the physical attraction is very real. The Bible says in 1 Corinthians 10:13 "No temptation has overtaken you that is not common to man. God is faithful, and he will not let you be tempted beyond your ability, but with the temptation he will also provide the way of escape, that you may be able to endure it." After running a few times and engaging him in the company of others, we finally had a conversation. I let him know that I was married, and although I found him attractive - the relationship could never be more than a friendship. *Submitting my body, mind, and spirit to the Lord helped me dodge that bullet <u>that</u> time, but it wouldn't stop the enemy from sending seductive arrows after me.*

Allure (noun) - the quality of being powerfully and mysteriously attractive or fascinating.

I had barely made it onto the train before I heard, "Doors Closing." As I moved to the car's center to hold onto something to keep from falling, I saw this guy that I had seen a few times in my office building. Smiling, he said, "Hello" and I simply responded, "Hey." That was our first encounter. We didn't have that much to say verbally, but our eyes connected, which can be dangerous. 1 John 2:16 states, *"For all that is in the world, the lust of the flesh, and the lust of the eyes and the pride of life, is not of the Father, but is of the world."* This is why most people don't give direct eye contact for a long period of time, because it's intimate. When we saw each other on the metro, we had conversations, which went on for a few weeks.

Then, he walked into my office. I started to act like a silly teenager and could feel "butterflies." He said, "Hello Ms. Lady," and I replied "Hello, Sir. I didn't know you worked on my floor." He had just started that week. As he walked out the door, he turned to me and said, "I guess we will be seeing a lot more of each other train buddy." With an encouraging smile, I replied, "I guess so, Sir". After that conversation, we saw each other in passing daily. We spoke about our dreams and also our fears. He listened and offered advice and support. For the first time in a long time, a piece of me that was dormant felt alive. I could hear lyrics playing in my mind from Fantasia's *When I See U (Fantasia.* Album. Prod. Midi Mafia, J, 19, 2007. Single).

> *"I scribble x and O's in my notebook. Checking how my hair and my nails look I feel myself in a zone I get nervous when you call So I say I'm not home I see your face And I hear my favorite song Should I send an e-mail at home? You're the number one topic on the phone I wonder if you know or do you have a clue, yeah I lay my head on my pillow. You got me staring out the window Wish on a star for a sign What's the reason why, yeah You're always on my mind When you come around I get shy. When I see you When I see you I never know when you might walk by So I gotta be right on time When I see you"*

On Fridays, we had longer conversations, and he would bring

me a cup of tea, a bagel with cream cheese, or lunch. These simple acts of kindness really made me feel appreciated, especially since I wasn't feeling that at home. I found myself rushing out to make it to see him on the train. I knew he would be waiting for me, and he always was. After a few months of these interactions, he asked for my number. I initially declined, but inevitably, I slipped it to him in passing. This friend and I often talked at night before going to bed. I would cuddle up on the couch and hold deep conversations with him, while my husband was in the room attending to his business.

Honey dip (noun, slang) – A pet name for someone you like.

I had interactions with men all the time, but nothing like this. I ignored all the warning signs and red flags. I knew my friendship had crossed a boundary and had become a threat not just to my marriage, but to my spiritual walk. I was being reckless, but I didn't care. In my mind, the marriage was over, and this friendship was a part of my "Exit Plan." I began to rationalize my actions. After all – didn't my husband have many years to change but did not? Why was *he* allowing another man to treat his wife better than *he* was? Hadn't *he* had friendships with other women? Our marriage had become more of a *business* partnership than a union anyway.

Unclean (adjective) – dirty; morally wrong; unfit to be consumed.

If my friend called and my husband was around, I would leave the room or let the phone go to voice mail. I would text him a response to say, "I'll call you later" or "I'm in a meeting and will contact you when I get out." I was looking for options and excuses to get away from my husband to get my emotional and fleshly fix. I was walking in self-deception. Since my husband and I were acting like business partners, it wasn't *really* a lie to say that I was in a meeting. I wasn't *really* doing anything wrong; we were *just* friends. I had informed this gentleman that I was in a complicated situation, but he literally and figuratively made the decision to ride the train.

My husband noticed a change in my attitude and patterns. Although I could see him watching when the phone rang or when I got late night calls, he didn't overtly question anything. I would drive by myself more. The things that used to bother me didn't even garner a response. The truth is, my joy was being restored with someone other than the man I married. I was having an ongoing interaction with someone and sharing some of my deepest emotions and thoughts. I didn't need to engage my husband anymore and I was perfectly fine with that. I had formed a closeness that stimulated me and had me wanting to give more. I had an emotional attachment with another man. I missed him when we didn't see each other, and soon our friendship moved beyond the work environment and public transportation. He was giving me the emotional support and attention I craved. We spoke about things beyond children, church, community activities, or monthly bills. We talked about things that not only inspired me, but stirred up passion. This newfound fascination and freedom were driving forces that kept me chasing this *Unclean Honey*.

Therefore judge nothing before the appointed time; wait until the Lord comes. He will bring to light what is hidden in darkness and will expose the motives of the heart. 1 Corinthians 4:5

      I had become comfortable in my secret life, but the truth always has a way of coming to light. I was scheduled to go to New York with my sister. I thought it would be a good time to get away to clear my mind, but I didn't get the chance. On the day of the trip, my husband confronted me about the phone calls that I had been having. He asked, "Who were you speaking with last night?" I replied, "A friend." "How did you meet this friend?" I could tell from his line of questioning that he knew more. He proceeded to tell me my friend's name and informed me that the two of them had a conversation. I was furious, but also a little frightened. At that moment, all I could think about is, "I wonder how my friend is feeling." My husband was shocked and upset. I told him I didn't have time for that and I had to get ready to leave. He said, "If you don't settle this today, I won't be here when you return." I was torn, because all the feelings for my husband I thought were dead came rushing back.

      I didn't want my husband to leave, but I wasn't ready to let go of my friend, either. I continued to rationalize and self-deceive. *My husband had played games for years, and now that someone else was interested, he was mad.* The conversation between my husband and me was not only heated, but very emotional. He asked me, "Did you sleep with him?" and I replied "NO"- which was the truth. We agreed to continue the conversation when I returned to give both of us time to process what had been revealed, and decide how we would move forward. I didn't contact my "FRIEND," because I knew that he was crushed. I had been lying and deceiving him, but later that evening, my friend sent me a message asking if I was OK and free to talk. He wanted to check on me, because he received a call from my husband and didn't know if I was a victim of domestic violence. I told him I was good. He asked, "Why didn't you tell me you were married?" I apologized and told him that the situation was complicated, and I really didn't expect us to develop feelings for each other. We decided to continue to be friends.

When I returned home, my husband and I had a very raw conversation. We discussed what led us to that place and how we could move pass it. My heart was cold, because I truly didn't know what would be different. He asked me, "Are you in love with this dude?" I replied, "I don't know, but he definitely has a part of my heart." I looked in my husband's eyes, and it seemed like his entire world came to an end. He knew if our marriage was going to be saved, he was going to have to fight for it. He went to speak with our Overseer to get guidance and prayer. At this point, I felt a release, because some things had been revealed, but secrecy and deception still flanked me on both sides.

The following Monday, my friend walked into my office with a butter pecan shake, my favorite. He wanted to take me out to dinner. Because I was still walking in secrecy, I didn't want anyone to see me out in public alone with another man. I also didn't want my friend to feel like my attitude had changed towards him, so I arranged for us to attend dinner. I invited an unsaved friend to join us, so I would be covered in case someone saw us. My behavior was escalating. I was walking in sin, and my witness was tarnished.

Many months had passed and my secret friendship had become a full-fledged emotional affair. The more I gave, the more he wanted. After all, he didn't know the whole truth. He knew I was married, but I told him that my husband and I were living as roommates. I started visiting him, but never went inside his home. I made sure these stops were quick, so I could account for any time with my husband. I was also thinking about my wedding vows. I knew if I had sex with this man, then my marriage was definitely over.

In spite of warnings from my close family and friends to work on my marriage, I continued on with my duplicity. Looking and smelling good, I finally decided to visit my friend alone. We had dinner on the patio, while we enjoyed the summer breeze and great conversation. It was getting late. I said, "I think I need to go." As I turned to leave, he embraced me and our eyes locked. He leaned in, and we engaged in a passionate kiss that landed us both against the front door. Our bodies were responding to the heat, and I had abandoned all caution! To my surprise, he pulled back and told me to go home. I did, but I had tasted the "HONEY" and it was indeed sweet. I continued to visit, but I never stayed that long again fearing what may happen. I started feeling convicted, because my husband was really trying to make it work. I knew that God couldn't repair our marital breach if I continued my unholy relationship, but I didn't know how to end it.

Eye Shadow

On one of my rendezvous, my friend said he had something to show me inside his Bible. He had placed my picture by Proverbs 18:22, which states: "He that findeth a wife, findeth a good thing," He told me he prayed for me daily and had also informed his family and friends about me. His dad wanted to meet the woman who was bringing his son so much joy, and his mom was praying for us. I was in disbelief. The weight and reality of this situation had finally hit me. This man is making plans to have a life with me, and I already have a life with someone else. I knew I had to end it quickly.

I put myself on the altar. I had to admit that although I hadn't engaged in sexual intercourse with my friend, we had an emotional affair. I asked my heavenly Father to forgive me for my transgressions, lies, and deceit. I bared my soul to Him and asked Him to break the emotional soul ties that I had with this man. I admitted my weakness and asked for help in ending the relationship. I asked God to relocate my friend to a place with a better job, and He did exactly that. I told Him if He did this for me, I would put the nail in the coffin.

As I lie on the floor in the fetal position, my Father began to speak and show me things concerning my relationship with my husband. He revealed all the anger, lies, fallacies, and extreme pain that my spouse and I would endure. He let me know that things would be extremely difficult and challenging. I couldn't understand why the Lord wanted me unhappy. Why was I not getting a release from this shipwreck of a marriage? I didn't want to go back into a tornado; I just wanted to be free! The LORD asked, "Do you trust me?" With snot dripping and tears running down my face, I replied "Yes." He said, "I'm not asking you to trust Greg; I'm asking you to trust me. I felt like the weeping Prophet Jeremiah when the Father stated to him, *"For I know the thoughts that I think toward you, said the LORD, thoughts of peace, and not evil, to give you an expected end."* (Jeremiah 29:11). After lying in my Father's arm for a few hours, I got up from the grave. I knew that whatever happened after that moment that God was with me, and that's all I needed to hear. I put on my big girl panties, and I arranged a meeting to end the love affair. I had to honor my word to the Lord.

On a warm summer night in July, at his going away party, I cut ties with my friend for good. With my eyes filled with tears and my heart racing, I went to see him. When he saw me, he knew immediately that it wasn't the visit he had planned. He said, "This is not what you really want. I can tell in your eyes that you're unhappy and deserve so much better." He embraced me, but with tears flowing down my face, I gently pulled away. I replied, "I'm so sorry. You are right, I am not happy, but my decision to leave can't be based on you. I have to give my marriage another chance. We have children, and a part of me still loves him despite what he has done to me. I was wrong for bringing you into this situation. I wasn't truthful with you. I should've told you I was married in the beginning, and you should've left when you found out. Goodbye." Leaving him standing there in pain that I had caused him, was one of the hardest things I've ever had to do.

The soul tie that I had with this other man really needed to be burned. I relied on God to give me the strength to be strong and obedient to Him. My spirit was telling me one thing, but my heart was telling me something totally different. A part of my heart was gone, but a little piece was holding on. I felt Jeremiah's pain when he said, "The heart is deceitful above all things, and desperately wicked: who can know it?" My heart was all over the place and emotionally attached to two men.

Foundation

     Walking away from a dilemma can be tricky if you're not focused and totally depending on the strength of the LORD, because you can find yourself back in a vicious love affair. The only person with the power to resolve the dilemma is the person who created it. God can and will make a means of escape for you, but it's your job to run when the door opens. This requires taking yourself and your flesh out of the equation and caring more about your spouse. You have to be dedicated to making your marriage work more than a night of pleasure or an expensive love affair.

     Emotional affairs usually start off innocent as it did for me, but they can be costlier than sexual affairs. An affair can be any ongoing secret encounter or interaction with someone who is not your spouse. The trouble starts when you do not maintain integrity and start living outside the boundaries of your marriage. When you find yourself walking in secrecy with phone calls, text messages, meetings, private chats, Face Time, or whatever you may be engaging in, you know that the friendship has crossed over to a dangerous place. I didn't just wake up this morning and say, "Today is the day I taste the "Unclean Honey" or "I think I want to start a love affair." We can all fall prey to the enemy if we don't protect our minds and hearts. If you are saying, "This will never happen to me," or "Our love is too strong for anyone to come between us," - think again.

     The journey to healing wasn't easy, but with the help of the Lord - it was obtainable. Healing from infidelity is hard, painful, and draining work; but if you both are committed to God, each other, and the process - you can survive. The weeks and months following the incident were awkward between my husband and me, because he could see me physically mourning for another man. He felt paralyzed with guilt, but found it hard to hide his frustration, anger, and hurt. We both had to bear witness to the fact that both of us had destroyed trust and caused pain. The journey to healing wasn't easy, but we made it through with the help of the Lord. Bouncing back from infidelity requires facing the heartache and aftermath that has been committed against the spouse and family. We both dealt with feelings of guilt and shame. *I* had to fully take responsibility for my own actions and not try to defend or deflect the impact my actions caused.

Following are some guidelines for helping to recover from an emotional affair. Of course, each situation is different, and other approaches, including seeking Christian counseling may be required.

1. Take responsibility. This is the first step to healing and is vital to the rebuilding of trust after a breach has occurred. You were not forced to cheat and must take full responsibility for your actions. In our case, we both had to step up to the plate. My husband had to take responsibility for his role in fostering an unhappy union. He knew the pain, hurt, and disappointment I was going through. He just continued on hoping it would disappear and I would continue going through the motions. Both of our actions created loneliness and isolation that compelled us to seek emotional intimacy outside the home.

2. Cease all communication with the outside party. In order to move forward, you must be willing to be transparent. Close the door to any relationship. This means not just physical contact, but no mail or electronic communications either. My recommitment to my marriage meant that I had to stop all communication with "Unclean Honey." You need to take the necessary steps to make your spouse feel safe and start to rebuild trust.

3. Reconnect with your spouse. Communication is the key to reconnecting. During the aftermath of an affair, it can be difficult. If you have a hard time expressing your feelings, you will need to push yourself beyond your comfort zone to save your marriage. It may be good to speak to a marriage counselor to help start the dialogue and release your feelings to your spouse. The last thing you want to do is lie, because you're afraid of your spouse's reactions. If the issue comes back later, it will be like starting the

process all over again. This will cause more distrust. You must also be willing to be on the spirit of longsuffering.

Understand there is no time frame for healing. When your spouse forgives you, it must be on his own time. Don't try to rush him through his process, because it's uncomfortable for you. Allow your spouse to process his anger, despair, tears, shock, and numbness. Being open and honest about what both of you are feeling will help build a stronger union. In due season, forgiveness and healing must emerge. Your marriage has a good chance of surviving infidelity and emerging strong if you can hold on and stay the course. Set aside some time for one another. During this time, don't talk about the marital breach, children, ministry, or anything that will get you sidetracked from each other. You will need a great support system, and people who are truly praying for you to get to work things out.

My husband and I learned to take care of each other again. In life, it's so easy to take care of the children, ministry, and others that we forget about taking care of the biggest gift God has given to us – each other. God not only rekindled our love, but He restored the years to our marriage. Now, we vow to keep it fresh! We not only choose to stay together, but set aside time to invest in our marriage, which is separate from marriage counseling or family time. We have date night at least three times a month. We come together to talk and enjoy each other. This gives us time to explore our relationship, goals, and just laugh.

Pastor Patricia Jackson
The Life Changing Church
4598 Beech Road
Temple Hills, Maryland 20748
www.thelifechangingchurch.org
301-702-2292
pastorpat@thelifechangingchurch.org

Patricia Jackson, fondly known as "Pastor Pat," is a woman of numerous talents, gifting's and abilities. A native Washingtonian, Pastor Pat is a highly sought after preacher, teacher and inspirational speaker. From her more than 35 years of ministry experience, Pastor Pat birthed the phenomenal teaching ministry, "Word of Life," which is impacting the lives of many people. She hosted her inaugural conference for Word of Life Ministries entitled, "Living An Amazing Life—Women Who Win, *#positionedforopendoors*, on October 24, 2015.

One of Pastor Pat's greatest desires is to see the lives of men and women changed for the better. She can often be heard telling people, "I just want you to be happy glad." One of the ways she strives towards this goal is by serving in the role of Co-Pastor of The Life Changing Church in Temple Hills, Maryland, alongside her husband, Bishop-Designate Herbert Jackson, Jr.

A person of extraordinary wisdom and business savvy, Pastor Pat is an entrepreneur, having interests in several businesses. She conducts these matters with great grace and vision while balancing the many responsibilities of motherhood. Pastor Pat is mother to two successful children, Whittney and H.J., both of whom are pursuing careers in the gospel music industry and their respective callings in ministry.

Pastor Pat's reach has always extended far beyond the four walls of the church. She served the needs of the community for many years as the Director of Residential Services for Covenant House Washington. In that capacity, she helped address the physical and emotional needs of at-risk youth.

Education serves as a top priority in Pastor Pat's life. She received her Bachelor of Arts Degree in Urban Studies, her Masters Degree in Divinity.

Throughout her life, she has held dear to her heart the Words our Lord Jesus Christ spoke as recorded in Matthew 6:33, "But seek ye first the Kingdom of God and His righteousness, and all these things shall be added unto you."

BEHIND THE MAKEUP

A MOST DEADLY DISEASE

Foundation

There is a disease that has critically plagued generation after generation, family after family, man, woman, boy, and girl. This disease has killed and continues to kill more people than cancer, HIV, heart attacks, or strokes. This disease has no respect of persons. It has crossed all racial barriers, and does not know gender, age or, economic status. This disease has been here since the world began. Adam and Eve suffered with this very disease and it caused the entire world to fall from the Grace of God (Gen. 3). Saul had this disease and it cost him his throne (1 Sam. 15:23-28). Eli had this disease and it cost him the most precious possession of that time, the Ark of the Covenant (the presence of God). Not only that, but Eli also lost his children and his own life (1 Sam. 4:10-18). Jonah had this disease and it caused him to think he could run from his assignment and hide from the Omniscient God. This disease cost him three days in the depths of the sea in the belly of a big fish (Jonah 1:17). This same disease caused David to sleep with Bathsheba and impregnate her. It caused him to setup and kill her husband, Uriah, so that he could have Bathsheba as his own wife, trying to disguise what was done in the dark. The consequences of David's actions cost the life of his first-born son with Bathsheba, and the pronouncement by the Prophet Nathan that killing and murder would continually plague his family forever. Lastly, this disease fueled Sampson's decision to negate his Nazarite vow and become involved with and be seduced by the harlot Delilah. This cost him his hair, his strength, his sight, and ultimately his life (Judges 16).

THIS DISEASE IS CALLED DENIAL!

Lipstick

I don't remember where I was coming from that night, nor do I remember the drive home. All I remember is that the street I was driving on was very dark and it seemed as though I was the only one on the street that night. I do know that up until that night I had been in DENIAL. I had been like an ostrich with my head in the sand. My mentality was if I deny what I see, it can't be true. "These kinds of things did not happen in my family." I had never known of any real tragedies, maybe some family fights back in the day, but never anything like this. I thought, any day now it would all be over, vanish and disappear. This thing would fix itself, or at some point I would wake up and things would be normal. After all, like they say, "Trouble don't last always." Deep down inside, I knew this was not a dream, and it was happening to me and my family. That night I had an awakening that seemed to come out of nowhere, and for the first time after seeing my husband month after month, struggling in his affliction, I knew he was dying. What I was facing was real and it was not going away. I had never felt so helpless in all of my life.

Webster's dictionary defines denial as a statement, saying that something is not true or real. It is defined as a condition in which someone will not admit that something sad, painful, etc., is true or real. Denial is a defense mechanism used by people to distance themselves from what is real or unpleasant or from some unacceptable behavior. When a person is in denial they unconsciously reject or block out reality. For example, a mother may reject the reality of her son or daughter being on drugs or a drug dealer. A wife or a husband may reject the reality that their spouse, is in an adulterous affair. A woman may reject the reality that she is in an abusive relationship. A man may reject that he is an abuser. An alcoholic will deny that they have a drinking problem. When a person is told that they have a terminal illness or in my case, which we will discuss later, that your loved one has a terminal illness and is going to die, the news can be so overwhelming that they enter into a state of denial. They refuse to accept the facts because it is too painful to handle.

The very thought that my husband would die, was too painful. Besides from accepting Christ, my husband was one of the best things that had ever happened in my life. Growing up in the hood in Northeast DC, did not offer many choices for a good husband or better yet, a decent life. Nevertheless, I had beat the odds and made it out of the "hood!" I had a good life, a good husband, and was raising a good family in a good Christian home. I had what many people in my family never had. As I drove home that night and as reality began to set in, I thought to myself, this is all I ever wanted, a good life. The threat that I would lose my husband and my children would be without a father was too much for me to bear. As a social service professional, and growing up in a home with an absent father, I knew all too well the plight of fatherless children. I knew what could happen to children growing up in single parent family households. This could not happen to me!

Like most of the enemy's tricks and traps, sometimes denial can be disguised as truth. Therefore, it is important in any situation, whether the bad news or potentially harmful situation, be our own or that of a loved one, that we know and understand the types of denial and the symptoms of denial so that what is false will not seem true. The Bible tells us that we perish because of a lack of knowledge (Hosea 4:6). Based on my own experience as a Leader and Pastor for the last 30 years, I know that many people are living in denial and have lived there for so long until the lie is reality to them. The fact of the matter is, denial comes to destroy, it is not a safety net, or a defense. Like the thief it is, it comes to kill, steal, and destroy (John 10:10). I also understand that when we are in denial, we are trying to save our life, but according to Luke 17:33, we are actually losing our lives. We become partners with the enemy to accomplish his mission.

Types of Denial

Denial does not come in just one form. There are several types of denial.

Denial of fact

- This form of denial utilizes deception. A person will use lies to avoid facts they think may be painful to themselves or others. Lies are told on purpose to cover up the truth. Their lies leave out pertinent facts in order to tailor a story to make it seem believable. People in this category will also sanction something to be true when it's really false.

Denial of responsibility

- This form of denial involves avoiding personal responsibility by:
    - blaming: the act or shifting the responsibility of a fault to someone or something other than the one responsible. I call this the "Blame Game."
    - minimizing: an attempt to make the effects or results of a situation appear to be less harmful or significant than it may actually be.
    - justifying: when someone attempts to make a situation or action seem right when it is actually wrong. The situation looks right because of their faulty perception of right and wrong.
    - regression: when someone is behaving in a manner that is immature for their age group (a woman may try to dress and act like a teenager because she is in denial about her age).

The bottom line is when someone is using denial of responsibility; they are usually attempting to avoid potential harm or pain by shifting attention away from themselves.

Denial of impact

- A person, who avoids understanding or thinking about the harm their behavior can cause to others or themselves, is operating in denial of impact. This way the person can avoid feeling a sense of guilt and thus prevents them from developing remorse or empathy for others. People who want to justify poor decisions use denial of impact to reduce or eliminate pain.

Denial of cycle

- There is a saying that says, "The definition of insanity is, doing the same thing over and over again and expecting different results. When a person avoids looking at their decisions or pattern of thinking and how harmful behavior is repeated, they are operating in denial of cycles. For example, a woman who keeps getting pregnant out of wedlock, may explain her behavior by saying things such as, "It just happened."

Denial of awareness

- Denial of awareness overlaps with denial of responsibility. It is an attempt to distract or distance oneself from the pain by claiming that they were unaware of their actions. This is very typical of drug addicts and alcoholics as well as some with mental health issues.

Denial of denial
- Denial of denial involves thoughts, actions, and behaviors which say that, "I'm ok and nothing in my personal behavior needs to change." Everyone else needs to change but not me. This type of denial involves self-delusion.

RECOGNIZING THE SIGNS OF DENIAL

Recognizing the signs of denial will not only help you, but someone you know who may be in denial. Sometimes the signs of denial may not be very obvious to you, the person in denial, or you may not recognize the signs in your loved one. The signs and symptoms of denial are:

Anger which can result when those that love you are trying to help you see reality;

Depression that comes at the very thought that what you refuse to own up to is really happening and there appears to be no help;

Immaturity because you refuse to take responsibility for actions or knowing the facts;

Hypertension which results from prolonged periods of stress because of denying the issues that are causing the stress; and,

Addictions because you rely on food, alcohol, drugs, gambling, shopping, sleeping, sex and other devices to feel better or to get through what you will not admit.

I displayed all of the symptoms. But my top three were anger, depression, and addictions.
During one of our ministry board meetings, a couple of days before the end of the meeting, my Bishop called me into conference. My husband did not attend the board meeting that year because he was on travel for his job to Japan. As I think back, in the back of my mind I knew he was too sick to travel. He later told me that he was so weak he could not even pull his own luggage. My Bishop took me into a private area and after some small talk (even in the small talk, I knew this conversation was not going to be good), she said to me, "Your husband is sick, very sick." In my state of denial, I became offended and would not allow the conversation to go where I thought she was taking it. "Oh, he's fine," I said interrupting her. "He's just tired and has been on a strict diet," although in reality he was eating everything in sight and losing weight rapidly. By this time, my husband had gone from 250 pounds to 180 pounds. After about two or three minutes of trying to help me see the urgency of the matter, she told me that we needed to face reality and take our heads out of the sand before it was too late. She had seen him a few months before the board meeting and had recognized a death spirit on him. Initially, when she called me in that room, I was not expecting her to confront me with the issue of my husband's affliction. This conversation took me totally by surprise. I didn't think anyone knew. I didn't think anyone saw what I pretended I did not see and refused to admit. I had completely shut out all of the talk and the whispers around the church. I convinced myself that they were talking about something else. I experienced all kinds of emotions that day. I

became very angry with my Bishop because I felt she had prophesied gloom and doom over my family. I left that board meeting that year never to return again. I never wanted to see her or anyone associated with her. I had one more day at the board meeting, but I wished that moment was the last day. I was ready to leave and the day of my departure could not come fast enough. One of the Elders from our church had accompanied me to the board meeting; she was also a very good friend and someone I trusted completely. We were sitting in the airport, on our way home, waiting to board our flight. By this time, I had gone from being angry to depressed. I could hardly lift my head and had I not been in the airport, I would have laid in the floor and cried profusely. I was in so much pain. I felt as though I was all alone without a friend in the world. Low self-esteem set in. I felt so insignificant and I began to doubt whether or not God loved me or cared. I needed to feel better, I needed peace. I wanted to tell my friend about the conversation that I had with my Bishop. I wanted to ask her if she thought the same about my husband, who was also her Pastor. I knew because of who she was, her integrity, her commitment to the ministry, and God as well as her love for my husband and me, she would tell me the truth. However, I was not ready to face the truth. Some years later, I asked her if she thought that my husband was sick. She told me that she had actually approached me about the situation. But to this day, I don't remember such a conversation. My friend said, not only did she think he was sick, the majority of the church that we pastored thought so and worried that if something did not happen soon we would be without a Pastor.

I could hardly wait to get home. All I wanted to do was pick up my children from the sitter and go home to my cozy little house, and everything would be fine. After all, this was just a "trick from the enemy" to stress me out. Well, when I arrived home, I immediately went to pick up my children, they were staying with a good friend. Then it happened again, "Pat, I need to talk to you about your husband," she said. I think I saw stars that day. Anger and resentment had flared up once again. I knew where she was going. I knew what she wanted to say. I turned to her and very sharply exclaimed, "I really appreciate your concern, but there is nothing to be concerned about, everything is fine, after all, sometimes things are not what they look like!" I immediately dismissed her and would not allow her to talk anymore about my husband. In addition to being angry and resentful, there I was minimizing the situation again and by this time I felt as if everyone was judging me and as a result, I had a major attitude with her, the church, and the world. I gathered up my children and went home.

My husband arrived home from Japan the next day after I arrived home from the board meeting. I remember seeing him struggle out of his car. He was so weak that he could hardly get up the steps to our house. Still in denial, I again minimized what I saw. He was just tired from his trip even though I could see that just after only a week, he had lost more weight. I refused to own up to what I knew deep down inside was the truth.

For the next few months, sugar became my best friend. It told me indulge, you'll feel better and that's what I needed. I ate most of the sugary things at night, because the sugar lows would help me sleep, sugar took me away from it all, it made me feel better. But like all addictions, feeling better was only temporary. I didn't really feel better, things got worse and I felt even worse. And added fifty more pounds to a very stressful body and the denial of a terminally ill husband was not a recipe for feeling better. It was a poison for gross obesity, hypertension, hair loss, borderline diabetes, and a potential nervous breakdown.

How long could I keep up this image that everything was alright? However, before I would finally face reality, I would experience one more symptom, immaturity. Because I refused to take responsibility for knowing the facts that were right before my face every day, I decided that if what my Bishop and my friend implied was true, when and if the big secret was ever revealed, I would just act surprised. I would pretend I knew nothing, had no idea, and it would be a shock. That was my plan and I was sticking to it.

Eye Shadow

The Power Of Truth

I had never thought of myself as a pretender. I always considered myself as being straight forward, out in the open, and transparent. Whereas the truth can be hard to face, pretending and living a lie is so much more difficult. The Bible says, there is a way that seems right to man, but in the end, it leads to destruction (Proverbs 14:12) and God knows I was on a fast track to destruction. That night on that dark road, something amazing happened to me. Everything came together, the voice of my Bishop, the voice of my sitter, the realization of the effect that my denial was having on my children and so for the first time I was willing to face the truth, my husband was dying. That night, the Grace of God intervened and overshadowed me, giving me the strength I needed to open my eyes to the truth that I had denied for months and the
wherewithal to face the many challenges that we would encounter in the months to come.

With tears rolling down my face, I had only one request, so with an audible voice I prayed, "God, don't let him die." I surrendered my state of denial. I decided to face my Goliath and fight.
I made a declaration, "I'm not going down like this!" This declaration would be my constant affirmation over the next two years, day in and day out. You see, sometimes things get worse before they get better. My husband had not been diagnosed at this point, but I decided that no matter what was wrong with him and in spite of the awful speculations, I would stand by him. I would become his voice and his strength.

The thing I realize now about being in denial is it was not so much that I did not think my husband was sick; I did not want to face up to why he was sick. Therefore, if I denied the sickness, then I could definitely deny why he was sick. What I was really trying to avoid is what people would say.

Facing the truth that I was in denial set me free from destruction, but not from trials, tribulation, and persecution. If I thought I was going through a nightmare before, well the coming months would seem like a tsunami. It's one thing to get an attack from your enemy, but it's a worse thing to get an attack from within your own camp. By this time, my husband was a whopping 138 pounds; he had seen several doctors and they were all baffled. Some of the ones in my camp who were not doctors but "friends of Job" knew exactly what was wrong and had the nerve to voice their diagnosis to me and my family and anyone else that would listen to them. Some of the people in the church gave my husband every sexually transmitted disease known to man. There were family members that I had not talked to in years that somehow found my phone number and called to say how sorry they were that my husband had infected me. There were those who I worked with in ministry who suggested that my husband was hiding his true identity and that I should get tested. There were people who suggested that it was okay for me to get a divorce. Whenever my husband and I went into public places and we ran into someone we knew, it turned into a very humiliating moment. People were afraid to touch us. People we had known for years avoided us. There were stares of disappointment and disgust. It was not only a humility season, but it was a shameful time. But the Grace of God helped me to withstand the naysayers, the spectators, and false accusers. The day I received truth and accepted what I denied; that my husband was dying, God and the whole host of heaven began to war on our behalf. I was clothed with the confidence that God was on my side. This new found confidence caused me to walk with my head held high in the very face of scandal, humiliation, and backstabbing. The talk and chatter I once avoided, I was now able to look in the face.
Turning away from denial to the truth ushered in strength and wisdom

beyond my years and experience. I received Grace not only to hold my head up high in the face of persecution; but in my husband's absence, I served as the Pastor of our church. I learned how to handle a potentially hostile takeover. Anyone seeking to Pastor a church soon learned, our church did not have a vacancy. Coupled with the wisdom of God and my husband's coaching from his bed of affliction, I successfully pastored the church and not one person left the church.

Accepting my denial not only strengthened me, but strengthened the Church. The Church now saw me as a strong leader who was determined to win in this battle. They joined forces with me and together we organized prayer groups for my husband. We all said the same things. We all believed God for my husband's complete healing. We were a force to be reckoned with. There were other long-time friends who would sponsor worship services. The money they raised helped strengthen our church's finances.

The Grace of God enabled me to maintain my employment as the Director of a transitional living program for teen mothers. As a mom, I never missed a beat. The children were clothed, fed, and homework was done. When I could not be with my children, there were support systems in place that I could trust. I maintained a B+ average while taking classes at the Bible college, where I later received my Masters of Divinity Degree. As a wife, I was the primary caretaker and advocate. Whenever my husband had an appointment, so did I. Our Primary care physician was always so impressed with our teamwork. We found favor with him and he made sure my husband was referred to the very best specialists.

Owning up to the truth forever changed me. I evolved from being, "The First Lady" to the Woman of God, the Ministry Gift to the Body of Christ. I was no longer fearful of what others thought or said. I came into the knowledge that I was so much stronger than I thought. It changed my relationship with my husband. We were already a close couple, but it grew us closer together. If we never knew it before, we came to know then that we had each other's back. It changed my relationship with my children. They felt safe and secure because they saw my confidence. It changed the way the church community saw me. They saw a strong woman committed to her marriage, her family, and to God. But most of all, it changed the way I saw me. Somewhere between the time I got married and became a mother, I, Patricia that outgoing, creative, spontaneous, forward thinking person, and the multi-tasker, had gotten lost. But, because I was forced to be all things to all people, I found me again. I'm not saying that all of this had to happen before I could find myself again, but God works all together for our good. Just think, all it took was facing my fears and overcoming the fact that I was in denial.

BREAKING FREE FROM DENIAL

We must understand that staying in denial could cost you your life, physically, mentally, spiritually, and emotionally, as well as the life of a loved one. It will prevent you from living the amazing and abundant life that Jesus promises in John 10:10. I recognized that night I had a lot to lose. Denial told me I was secure and needed to protect my life by living a lie. In actuality, I was losing everything I had ever hoped for.

If I had to give a turning point for me coming out of denial, it was when I realize what my being in denial was doing to my children. My husband and son have always had a very close relationship and during the time of my husband's affliction, he slept a lot. I minimized it and brushed it off as him being tired. My husband's sleeping a lot hindered his interaction with our son. Because my son was not able to interact with his father, I saw my son's spirit begin to wither Having limited interaction, caused my son, a very vibrant, outgoing, inquisitive, full of life little boy, to begin to turn inward. He became very sad and withdrawn. It was as if he disappeared in the background. If my husband was away from us for longer than a work day, he would ask, "Is daddy coming?" My daughter, well, like mother, like daughter. She took on my posture of denial. She saw, but she didn't see. His death would have been absolutely devastating to her. I remember praying and saying to God, "Lord you have to let him live. He has a son, and I don't know how to raise a man. He's spoiled his daughter rotten and she would turn the funeral out." He told the people at The Life Changing Church, the assignment you gave him, that they were going somewhere; and, if you let him die, you would be a liar. When I think that my being in denial could have negated all of what God wanted to do, it makes me repent and wish I had recognized my state of mind earlier on.

I can't tell you that coming out of my state of denial was easy. Breaking free takes courage and maturity. However, it will be worth it. It is my prayer that this testimony will help you or someone you know and love to recognize that being in denial can and will destroy their life. I pray that God will give you or your loved one the strength and the courage to break free of this deadly disease called DENIAL.

Oh, by the way, I never mentioned my Husband's diagnosis, who is COMPLETELY HEALED. Well, that's his story! Be on the lookout for the book.

PRINCIPALS FOR BREAKING FREE FROM DENIAL

Listed below are some principles that helped me break free of denial:

1. Think about the potentially negative consequences of not taking action. Continuing in denial will cost you, as well as others.

2. Journal: Be honest with yourself and write down what you honestly feel. Examine what you really fear about the situation. God is not intimidated by our conversations with Him. He welcomes our questions, our frustrations, and our concerns.

3. Proceed with caution on this one, but confide in a trusted friend, or a loved one who can help you deal with stressful situations and provide suggestions for healthy ways to cope with the situation rather than trying to pretend it doesn't exist.

4. Last, but not least, Pray. Pray honestly. God already knows what you are going through. God is with you even in the valley and He's building stairs to get you out.

REFLECTIONS

1. After reading my story, can you admit that you or someone you love is in denial?

2. What do you think the denial is about?

3. Can you identify with any of the types of denial; and if so, in what category of denial do you or your loved one fall and why?

4. What are the denial symptoms?

5. What steps can be taken to move past the denial?

6. Once you or the person moves past denial what do you think the outcome will be?

Co-Pastor Michelle D. Limes
The City of David Ministries
7842 Parston Drive
Forestville, MD 20745
www.tcodm.org
copastormichelle@tcodm.org
(301) 200-CITY (2489)

BEHIND THE MAKEUP

Co-Pastor Michelle D. Limes has a mandate by God to preach and teach the gospel and is anointed to bring deliverance through the Word of God in clarity and simplicity. God uses her to heal, and break cycles of bondage.

She is a cutting edge, radical woman of God that believes that "the power of God can break any stronghold over your life; if you let Him." "You do not have to stay in the place that you're in!"

Co-Pastor is the wife of Pastor R. Sean Limes of the City of David of Ministries, of Forestville, MD. They are under the leadership of Bishop Glen A. Staples, Senior Pastor and Presiding Prelate of the Temple of Praise International Fellowship Churches.

Co-Pastor Limes attended Maple Springs Bible College and in May 2001 she received her license to minister and was ordained in October of 2004.

Co-Pastor Michelle is the CEO and Founder of WAKE UP! an movement to for women to ignite them to walk in their Kingdom destiny in every area of their lives by way of social skills development, counseling, restoration sessions, workshops and worship services.

Co-Pastor Limes is a native Washingtonian and has three wonderful children, Marcus, Aaron and Ashlee.

As she stands on the Psalm 91:1 "He that dwelleth in the secret place of the most High shall abide under the shadow of the Almighty." She knows she must lean and depend on God for everything. "He is the source of my strength and faith is not faith until it's tested."

"God has released unto me my assignment and now it's time to rediscover, redeem and ignite my dreams, goals and God-given purpose!

"God has released unto me my assignment and now it's time to rediscover, redeem and ignite my dreams, goals and God-given purpose!"

OF A LEADING LADY

GETTING BACK TO MY HAPPY PLACE
OVERCOMING THE SPIRIT OF DEPRESSION

Foundation

The last few years have been life changing for me. I have learned a lot of lessons and defeated many traps that the enemy has set up for my demise, one of which is the spirit of depression.

One instrumental thing I learned about the spirit of depression is that the enemy wants you to stay silent; however, turning it from a private focus on self, to corporate worship of Christ, can only defeat depression. The Word of the Lord says in Matthew 11:28-30 "Jesus said, "Come to Me, all you who are weary and burdened, and I will give you rest. Take My yoke upon you, and learn from Me, because I am gentle and humble in heart, and you will find rest for your souls. For My yoke is easy, and My burden is light"

God is inviting us to give our burdens to Him! Depression *is* a spirit, a disease sent to afflict the body and torment the mind by taking control over your thoughts. The spirit of depression doesn't travel alone; it has companions. It comes in like a dark, heavy cloud. And this cloud of depression is not mental, but spiritual. It is called the spirit of heaviness. *"To appoint unto them that mourn in Zion, to give unto them beauty for ashes, the oil of joy for mourning, the garment of praise for the spirit of heaviness; that they might be called trees of righteousness, the planting of the Lord, that he might be glorified."* Isaiah 61:3.

In the Bible, this spirit is called a strongman. *"But if I cast out devils by the Spirit of God, then the kingdom of God is come unto you. Or else how can one enter into a strong man's house, and spoil his goods, except he first bind the strong man? and then he will spoil his house."* Matthew 12:28-29.

Eye Shadow

Before the spirit of depression even enters the mind, other spirits are at work to manipulate your thoughts, attitude, and character. Oftentimes, we don't pay attention; we simply accept the behavior because we believe it to be justified. The Bible says, *(Proverbs 23:7) "For as he thinketh in his heart, so is he: Eat and drink, saith he to thee; but his heart is not with thee."*

These spirits attach themselves and work on your emotions. It's why many times, you "feel" something is not right, but don't always know what that something is or why you feel that way. You are being manipulated and set up by the spirit of depression, to get control over your mind, and steal your joy.

The spirit of depression wants you to keep silent and internalize. When we internalize emotions like bitterness, anger, sadness, and loneliness; spreads like a cancer. It's time to declare your healing and not keep silent! Open your mouth and tell God all about it. As you begin to reclaim your mind, peace, and happiness back from the enemy, he will not want to release you without a fight. You will have go to into battle and fight against his lies and confusion. You must pray and ask God to give you a sound mind according to 2 Timothy 1:7 "For God did not give us a spirit of fear, but of power and of love and of a sound mind!" God has given you the power and authority to experience to true joy, restoration, and freedom!

Lipstick

For me the spirit of depression took a very subtle approach. Two years ago, I was diagnosed of kidney cancer. I initially went to the ER for abdominal pain. After several tests, doctors performed a CT Scan and a tumor was revealed. The next two weeks were daunting. I had two surgeries 20 days apart, one on my kidney, the other a full hysterectomy. Everything happened so fast that I really did not know how to feel. But I kept my trust in God. During the healing process, I kept asking God what was I supposed to learn from this whole experience, and all that He would say is, "My Grace is Sufficient."

This was my sixth surgery during a 5-year time frame. The hysterectomy threw my body into full menopause. My weight went up and down, and my hair began to come out because of medication. Even though my husband was very supportive, I still felt alone and like no one truly understood what I was feeling. So I suppressed my feelings, put on the happy face, and dealt with it. After four weeks of bed rest, I went back to church. I continued to preach, teach, and pray for others. I continued to pastor and counsel, and witnessed manifestations of people being delivered. Everything was back to normal – or so I thought.

I realized, as time went on, that I did not like this "new body." The physical and emotional fluctuations due to the surgeries angered me. My self-esteem was low and I was tired, but I prayed and believed God for a change.

Let's put a pin right here….people must understand that just because you have a title: "Pastor, Co-Pastor, Apostle, etc," does not mean you don't go through. In fact, you go through even the more! I was suffering emotionally and physically. Yes, I believed God. Yes, I trusted Him. But at the same time, I was weak and had deep-rooted issues that needed to be dealt with. Through my afflictions, I learned some things about myself. God showed me my issues were fear of abandonment and rejection. I believe when we deal with deep-rooted issues, it usually stems from our childhood years. The fear of abandonment and rejection issues developed through being a fatherless child – always feeling I would be left alone. My father died when I was two weeks old.

The parent-child relationship is the first connection we experience. I never experienced a father's love. In the past, most of my relationships with men suffered because of it. This issue also spilled into my marriage. Even though my husband constantly told me I was beautiful, I could not receive it. So I continued to suppress my feelings and resentments and dealt with it. After all, my family needed me as well as the church. I did not take time to sort out my life; I was busy being available to others. We women have a tendency to take care of everybody else and put ourselves on the back burner. I was clearly hurting but covered it with ministry and other people's needs.

One year later, I suffered 2nd and 3rd degree burns on my upper torso due to a pressure cooker explosion. I went into a state of shock and did not realize what had really happened. My husband came home minutes later and took me to the hospital. I had to have an emergency surgery……..yet again. This time skin grafts/skin rearrangements. After my hospital stay, I had to be taken care of at home. My husband became my caregiver, cleaning my wounds and changing my bandages every night. I felt so ugly and was in so much pain. I was an emotional wreck! I did not want to leave the house, I did not want to look at myself in the mirror, and I would not be intimate with my husband unless the lights were out because I was ashamed of my body. I did not even want to see my own body in the shower. I sunk into a state of depression. Even though my husband never complained and always spoke words of life to me, it was not about how he felt about me; it was about how I felt about myself.

Just getting up or getting dressed in the morning was drudgery. I was always tired, exhausted, and fatigued. I slept to avoid the emotional pain. I wanted to be alone. I was angry and became bitter. I became angry when people would say, "Why are you tripping over some burns? At least you didn't get burned on your face." Tired of hearing, "You are a pastor. You will be alright. Just pray!" I was praying, *and* reading God's Word, but I just could not shake it! So I continued to mask my pain with work.

Through all this, God graced me to continue to minister, pray, and help others while I was denying myself the truth of what was really happening with me. Hiding my condition did not make it go away. I knew this was a serious battle of spiritual warfare.

I had to fight for my life, fight for my sanity, and fight for my peace and joy! I was not the woman God purposed me to be. I was hiding behind ministry, home, children, family, and the cares of life, and not tending to my own needs and issues. I stopped taking care of myself; I just really did not care anymore. I manage to hide my condition from my husband, family, and the people closest to me. Constantly covering up, I guess I indirectly hid it from myself. The Lord was pulling on me saying, "I'm in need of you." But I would not respond. How many know that obedience is better than sacrifice? I needed to shake myself. I needed to apply what I knew the Word of the Lord was saying to me. I was already in a low place and before I knew it, here came another traumatic situation.

When the enemy attacks children, it is always hurtful for the parents to endure. Even though God had His hand on my child, I became totally consumed with the problem and continued to ignore my own. I was so consumed that one day I blacked out in a hospital garage and did not know where I was. Truth be told, I didn't know *who* I was. I was not myself and realized I had not been myself for a long time.

As Pastors we are commissioned to make ourselves available for the people of God. I wanted God to be pleased with me as a leader. I was a new Pastor and I wanted to cross every T and dot every I; I just wanted to fulfill my

God-given assignment. But I learned the hard way that by not taking care of me, I would never be able to truly be effective for someone else. So I finally got tired to feeling defeated; I was tired to crying and feeling sorry for myself.

I asked God to deliver me from the Spirit of heaviness and put on the Garment of Praise. I confessed to Him how I truly felt; I repented for not being obedient. The Lord forgave me and spoke in my spirit Proverbs 3:6 "Seek his will in all you do, and he will show you which path to take." The Lord did exactly what His Word said and my healing journey began.

Through prayer and fasting, God gave me the power to finally break free from the subtle destroyer of depression and reclaim a life of passion and purpose. If allowed, depression can squeeze the joy out of your worship and prayers. It can pressure you to keep quiet when God wants you to speak up. And it can steal the peace of knowing that you belong to God.

Understand this, going through trials and tribulations are inevitable; but how we go through is the key. We can't give up the fight because God has given us the POWER! Just like 1Peter 5:10 "And after you have suffered a little while, the God of all grace, who has called you to his eternal glory in Christ, will himself restore, confirm, strengthen, and establish you." Through all I went through – the suffering, the Lord restored, confirmed, strengthened, and established me. So I suffered, but I WON!! My suffering was purposeful.

I had to get to a place where I had to see myself the way the Lord saw me and walk in it!! He allowed everything I went through, but I must admit, it made me stronger, wiser, and better. I have a deeper understanding of how to deal with tactics of the enemy. The enemy tried to stop my purpose by bogging me down with unhealthy emotions, but through God's Love and His Word He taught me how to manage them and gave me freedom. It all begins with the mind. Make up in your mind not to give up! According to Colossians 3:2, set your mind on things above and keep it set! The mind is a major key to overcoming depression. What you think about has the power to affect every area of your life. That's why we must renew our minds with the promises found in God's Word.

We can't control our circumstances, and we will never be completely free from experiencing pain or disappointment, but we don't have to let what happens today ruin our tomorrow. We must learn in all things we must rest in God – depend on Him for every part of our lives. We can't do anything in our own strength and leave God out of the equation. We must lean on God, no matter what our circumstances may be.

Remember the devil is a LIAR!! All he does is LIE! God has given us the power to fight according to Ephesians 6:12 "For we are not fighting against flesh-and-blood enemies, but against evil rulers and authorities of the unseen world, against mighty powers in this dark world, and against evil spirits in the heavenly places."

If you or someone you know is battling the spirit of depression, to experience deliverance one must first meditate on the Word of the Lord.

When you read the Word of God it renews your spirit, and refreshes your mind.

Below I have provided some scriptures for meditation:

(Isaiah 26:3) "Thou wilt keep *him* in perfect peace, *whose* mind *is* stayed *on thee:* because he trusteth in thee."

(Romans 12:1, 2) "I beseech you therefore, brethren, by the mercies of God, that ye present your bodies a living sacrifice, holy, acceptable unto God, *which is* your reasonable service. And be not conformed to this world: but be ye transformed by the renewing of your mind, that ye may prove what *is* that good, and acceptable, and perfect, will of God."

(Ephesians 4:23) "And be renewed in the spirit of your mind;"

(John 14:27) "Peace I leave with you, my peace I give unto you: not as the world giveth, give I unto you. Let not your heart be troubled, neither let it be afraid."

(Philippians 4:6-7) Be careful for nothing; but in every thing by prayer and supplication with thanksgiving let your requests be made known unto God. And the peace of God, which passeth all understanding, shall keep your hearts and minds through Christ Jesus."

(Philippians 4:8, 9) Finally, brethren, whatsoever things are true, whatsoever things are honest, whatsoever things are just, whatsoever things are pure, whatsoever things are lovely, whatsoever things are of good report; if there be any virtue, and if there be any praise, think on these things. Those things, which ye have both learned, and received, and heard, and seen in me, do: and the God of peace shall be with you.

(Joshua 1:6-9) Be strong and of a good courage: for unto this people shalt thou divide for an inheritance the land, which I swear unto their fathers to give them. Only be thou strong and very courageous, that thou mayest observe to do according to all the law, which Moses my servant commanded thee: turn not from it to the right hand or to the left, that thou mayest prosper withersoever thou goest. This book of the law shall not depart out of thy mouth; but thou shalt meditate therein day and night, that thou mayest observe to do according to all that is written therein: for then thou shalt make thy way prosperous, and then thou shalt have good success. Have not I commanded thee? Be strong and of a good courage; be not afraid, neither be thou dismayed: for the Lord thy God is with thee whithersoever thou goest.

Conclusion:

You can defeat the spirit of depression by not being enticed into believing what the enemy speaks to the mind. Don't give in to it and don't allow any of these things to defeat you! Continue to push to succeed in every aspect of life, while you have the opportunity to pursue your visions and dreams.

Pray without ceasing, keep God first, and remember whatever you may go through, "Count it all joy, my brothers, when you meet trials of various kinds, for you know that the testing of your faith produces steadfastness. And let steadfastness have its full effect, that you may be perfect and complete, lacking in nothing." James 1:1-4a.

THANK YOU

For Purchasing Your Copy Of Behind The Makeup Of A Leading Lady. We hope you have enjoyed reading each of our testimonies of hope.

ALSO AVAILABLE

BEHIND THE MAKEUP (The First Book in the collection)

Visit us on the Web to find out more at
www.behindthemakeup.org

Credits:
Photo credit Scott Midgett
Big Shot Scott Photography- www.Bigshotscott.com

Photo Credit Acquanette Daniel aquatonedan@yahoo.com

Editing Services by Angela McClain AM Editing amediting35@gmail.com

www.ingramcontent.com/pod-product-compliance
Lightning Source LLC
Chambersburg PA
CBHW050650160426
43194CB00010B/1882